Vol. V  No. 1

# Adult Bible Class
## Large-Print Edition

**WINTER QUARTER**  December 2013, January, February 2014

Editorial .................................................................................................................. 2

### Jesus and the Just Reign of God
#### UNIT I: Sending Jesus

| | |
|---|---|
| Dec. 1—Jesus' Birth Foretold—Luke 1:26-40 ............................................................ | 4 |
| Dec. 8—Mary's Song of Praise—Luke 1:46-56 .......................................................... | 9 |
| Dec. 15—Zacharias's Prophecy—Luke 1:57, 67-79 ................................................... | 14 |
| Dec. 22—Jesus' Birth (Christmas)—Luke 2:1-17 ...................................................... | 19 |
| Dec. 29—Jesus Presented in the Temple—Luke 2:25-38 ......................................... | 24 |

#### UNIT II: Ushering in the Reign of God

| | |
|---|---|
| Jan. 5—Honoring the Sabbath—Luke 6:1-11 ........................................................... | 29 |
| Jan. 12—Living as God's People—Luke 6:20-31 ...................................................... | 34 |
| Jan. 19—Showing Humility—Luke 14:7-14 ............................................................... | 39 |
| Jan. 26—Instruction on True Wealth—Luke 16:19-31 ............................................... | 43 |

#### UNIT III: Living Justly in the Reign of God

| | |
|---|---|
| Feb. 2—Hear and Do the Word—Jas. 1:19-27 ......................................................... | 47 |
| Feb. 9—Avoid Showing Favoritism—Jas. 2:1-13 ...................................................... | 51 |
| Feb. 16—Show Your Faith by Your Works—Jas. 2:14-26 .......................................... | 55 |
| Feb. 23—Control Your Speech—Jas. 3:1-12 ............................................................ | 59 |
| Paragraphs on Places and People ......................................................................... | 63 |
| Daily Bible Readings .............................................................................................. | 64 |

Editor in Chief: Grace M. Todd

Edited and published quarterly by
**THE INCORPORATED TRUSTEES OF THE GOSPEL WORKER SOCIETY
UNION GOSPEL PRESS DIVISION**

Rev. W. B. Musselman, Founder

Price: $3.15 per quarter*
$12.35 per year*
*shipping and handling extra

ISBN 978-1-936898-18-3

Lessons based on International Sunday School Lessons; the International Bible Lessons for Christian Teaching, copyright © 2010 by the Committee on the Uniform Series and used with permission. Edited and published quarterly by The Incorporated Trustees of the Gospel Worker Society, Union Gospel Press Division, 2000 Brookpark Road, Cleveland, Ohio 44109-5812. Mailing address: P.O. Box 6059, Cleveland, Ohio 44101-1059. www.uniongospelpress.com

**EDITORIAL**

# God Reigns

STEVEN D. PYLE

From the time we are children, we are concerned with justice. Just listen to a playground discussion (or is it an argument?) about the lack of fairness in some activity. Of course, concern about what is right is not the exclusive domain of children. Have you ever heard a discussion about the fairness of an umpire's call?

Try as we may, though, fairness—or justice—is not something human beings are good at. Look at the insider trading and other financial scandals that plague us. If you are into sports, look at how some athletes try to subvert what is right by using performance-enhancing drugs or trying to rig games for their own benefit.

However, with God there is no problem of justice. Through Jesus we have received guidance in how to live. God reigns and will continue to reign, and it is through Him we learn to live in His kingdom. The question is whether His justice is evident in people's lives or they live separated from His justice and possibly, eternally, from Him.

God sent Jesus to bring His reign to the lives of mankind. Jesus' birth was foretold through the Old Testament Scriptures. Throughout the years there was some knowledge of God's promise of a Messiah, but no one really knew when that day would come. It was to Mary in Nazareth that it was revealed when the Son of God would enter into the stream of human history. No longer was the event at some indeterminate time. It was now nine months in the future.

Mary recognized that God was introducing a blessed event, and she praised His name. Zacharias and Elisabeth were blessed as well by the promise of a son, and they too praised God. At the birth of his son, Zacharias praised God both for his son and for the redemption of Israel. John would go on to become the forerunner of Mary's Son—the Messiah.

What a blessed occasion it was when Jesus was born! Lest we forget, it was not to be the high and mighty who would receive the revelation of the Messiah. It was not the proud to whom the birth was revealed. It was to humble shepherds watching their sheep that the angels announced the birth of Jesus. The shepherds were simply going about their usual activities.

About a month and a half later, other individuals were going about what they usually did when the firstborn Son of Mary was presented to the Lord in the temple in keeping with what was called for in the Jewish Scripture. It was there that Simeon and Anna came to behold the Child. They praised God for sending the Messiah.

When Jesus ministered on earth, He taught many things that were near to God's heart. One thing that God desires is for His people to truly observe a day of worship and rest. But that day should not be lost in a maze of rules and regulations. We should be prepared to do what is good on Sunday. In addition to our usual time of worship, this could include helping a person with a flat tire whom we happen to see on the way home from church or visiting someone at the hospital.

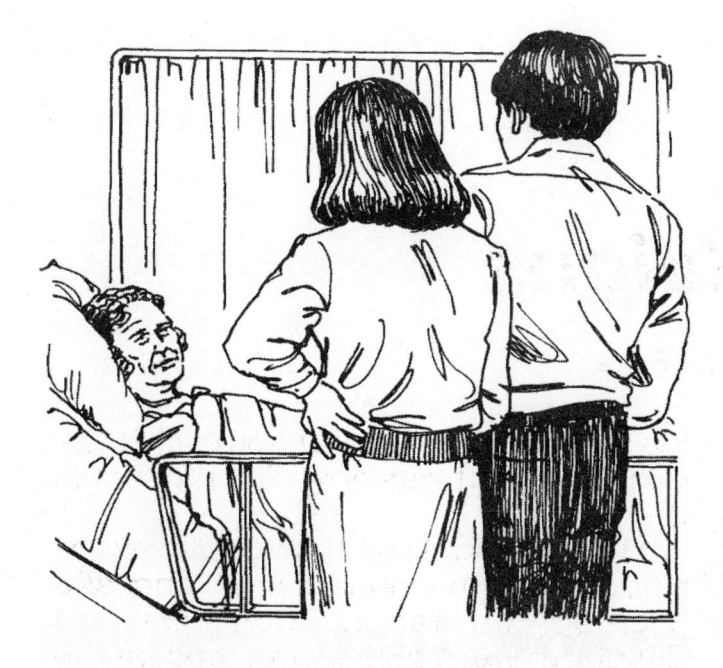

In whatever believers are doing, they need to serve humbly. If they trumpet their efforts for all to see, that may be all the honor they ever see. Jesus told us that the one who serves in a spirit of humility will be rewarded by God.

God desires that we recognize that all we need to know for salvation and living in Him has been revealed to us in His Word. One of the places where some foundations for living in God's kingdom are revealed is in the book of James.

A citizen in God's kingdom will seek to do certain things. Of course, we will be successful at these things only if we allow God's power to fill us and help us live justly.

God desires Christians to go beyond reading His Word and even being able to tell others what we have learned. God wants us to do what we have read about and know. That includes not showing partiality, whether based on economic status, social acceptability, racial distinctions, or educational differences.

If we claim that we have faith but do not have actions to show that our faith is real, then (as James writes) our faith is dead. That includes examples provided in James 2:15-20, as well as every area of our lives. This is what it means to live by faith.

But all this will be undone if we do not control our speech. Look around you. How often have the actions of a person been negated by the words he spewed forth? Does someone not appear as friendly or fair after he opens his mouth?

Do we proclaim the peace and unity that God sets forth and then fuss and fume because of an event at an athletic contest or loudly insist on our rightness in something that is ultimately trivial? Maybe our perception of God's reign has been detoured from the truth by our buying into a corrupt world and its philosophy.

Of even more concern is how we interact with God. Do we complain about a rainy day and then turn around and thank God for our food when He was the One who also gave us the rainy day? There is something wrong with this. James's illustration is appropriate here. Indeed, this should not be! Both streams of thought should not come from the same source.

Ask God to help you control your tongue. Ask Him to enable you to get the attitude behind those words to be one of praising Him always. Make time right now to ask Him to help you live as a citizen in His just kingdom.

Adult Bible Class

LESSON 1                                    DECEMBER 1, 2013

# Scripture Lesson Text

**LUKE 1:26** And in the sixth month the angel Ga′bri-el was sent from God unto a city of Gal′i-lee, named Naz′a-reth,

**27 To a virgin espoused to a man whose name was Jo′seph, of the house of Da′vid; and the virgin's name** *was* **Ma′ry.**

28 And the angel came in unto her, and said, Hail, *thou that art* highly favoured, the Lord *is* with thee: blessed *art* thou among women.

**29 And when she saw** *him,* **she was troubled at his saying, and cast in her mind what manner of salutation this should be.**

30 And the angel said unto her, Fear not, Ma′ry: for thou hast found favour with God.

**31 And, behold, thou shalt conceive in thy womb, and bring forth a son, and shalt call his name JE′SUS.**

32 He shall be great, and shall be called the Son of the Highest: and the Lord God shall give unto him the throne of his father Da′vid:

**33 And he shall reign over the house of Ja′cob for ever; and of his kingdom there shall be no end.**

34 Then said Ma′ry unto the angel, How shall this be, seeing I know not a man?

**35 And the angel answered and said unto her, The Ho′ly Ghost shall come upon thee, and the power of the Highest shall overshadow thee: therefore also that holy thing which shall be born of thee shall be called the Son of God.**

36 And, behold, thy cousin E-lis′a-beth, she hath also conceived a son in her old age: and this is the sixth month with her, who was called barren.

**37 For with God nothing shall be impossible.**

38 And Ma′ry said, Behold the handmaid of the Lord; be it unto me according to thy word. And the angel departed from her.

**39 And Ma′ry arose in those days, and went into the hill country with haste, into a city of Ju′da;**

40 And entered into the house of Zach-a-ri′as, and saluted E-lis′a-beth.

# Jesus' Birth Foretold

## Lesson: Luke 1:26-40

Read: Luke 1:26-45

TIME: 7 or 6 B.C.             PLACE: Nazareth

---

**GOLDEN TEXT** — "Behold, thou shalt conceive in thy womb, and bring forth a son, and shalt call his name JESUS" (Luke 1:31).

---

## Lesson Exposition

**GABRIEL'S COMING — Luke 1:26-29**

**Gabriel in Nazareth (Luke 1:26).** Situated in lower Galilee (relatively distant from the Sea of Galilee and the town of Capernaum, which was so important in the career of Jesus), Nazareth was an unlikely home for Messiah's family. Galilean towns tended to have populations in the range of five hundred to a thousand people; Nazareth, based on incomplete site surveys, was smaller still. It was not a place expected to produce great stirrings of messianic redemption.

**Mary, the betrothed (Luke 1:27).** "Mary," which in Hebrew appears as "Miriam" or "Maryam," was the most common Jewish name for women in our sources from that time in the land of Israel. Luke emphasized in his manner of telling the story that she was unmarried and a virgin, since this is a vital issue in understanding not only what happened to Mary but also the nature of Messiah as the God-Man.

Being espoused, or betrothed, in Jewish life meant a bond as certain as marriage but without the marital rights of cohabitation. Breaking a betrothal was as serious as getting divorced (Matt. 1:19).

Jesus is called "Son of David" sixteen times in the New Testament. This is especially a title used by Matthew. Paul referred to Him, in good Jewish manner, as "made of the seed of David according to the flesh" (Rom. 1:3). Of course, the long-awaited Messiah had to come from the line of David according to numerous prophecies, such as Isaiah 11:1. Through His legal father, Joseph, Jesus was descended directly from David. Many have theorized as well (though the New Testament does not confirm it) that Mary too was of David's line. Joseph is referred to explicitly as Jesus' father in Luke 2:48, as well as in the genealogy in 3:23. Furthermore, it was always the father's house that determined tribal lineage in Israel. Jesus was a son of David (and the Son of David) through His father, Joseph.

**An angel's blessing (Luke 1:28).** Gabriel's greeting to Mary was a blessing, a statement of an important development coming from the divine hand in Israel. As we read his words, the smallness of Nazareth, the young age of Mary, and the seeming insignificance of the scene all seem to recede into the background. We are now looking at the place where heaven meets earth. Mary

Adult Bible Class      5

remains, quite literally, the most blessed of all women who have ever lived. No mother has ever had such a child or conceived in such a manner.

**An Israelite's awe (Luke 1:29).** The ordinariness of the people God uses is often emphasized in Scripture. We tend to imagine that the Bible characters who were used for important things were ideal people or beyond human in some way. Mary was very young and unmarried, and being greeted by a stranger was out of the ordinary! Based on similar angelic visits in Genesis and Judges, it is likely that Gabriel appeared simply as a man.

Luke does not say that Mary was in awe or fear because Gabriel's glory was evident. She was fearful and awed because the greeting was unthinkable in its clear meaning. Who was Mary to imagine herself the most blessed of women?

## GABRIEL'S ANNOUNCEMENT—Luke 1:30-33

**A son named Jesus (Luke 1:30-31).** Ordinary people whose lives intersect with momentous happenings in God's plan often need to be told, "Fear not." This troubling incident, which was about to become more alarming as the scope of Mary's role was revealed, was for the good.

In fact, instead of being distressed, Mary needed to know that she was favored by God. "Favor" and "grace" are related words. Was Mary favored because she was a fitting person to be the mother of Messiah, or was this favor beyond what any person could deserve? Most likely both are true. To become the mother of Messiah was a blessing few women would dream of, but Mary was no doubt chosen as a person of faith and devotion.

**His greatness and kingdom (Luke 1:32-33).** The greatness of Messiah is explained in terms from the Old Testament, drawing the mind of the reader to the origins of the Messiah concept. The king from whose line Messiah would come was David. Before David was born, prophecies about him also looked ahead to Messiah (cf. Gen. 49:10; Num. 24:17).

To David, God said, "Thine house and thy kingdom shall be established for ever before thee" (II Sam. 7:16). Gabriel announced Jesus as the fulfillment of this, since He will be King over Jacob forever.

## MARY'S CONCERN—Luke 1:34-37

**A virginal conception (Luke 1:34-35).** Like the wife of Manoah (Judg. 13), Mary received an angelic announcement of a special birth to occur shortly in her future. Mary's situation, however, was different in one most radical way. No mere words can describe the unparalleled circumstances of this conception. The strange words of Isaiah 7:14, uttered more than seven hundred years before Mary, had not prepared anyone to understand what was happening. Mary realized immediately what seemed wrong with the announcement she received from God: how could a virginal maiden conceive?

Gabriel's answer is in poetic form, like the Psalms, using parallelism. The Spirit would come upon Mary, and the power of the Highest would overshadow her. The Spirit had come upon people many times—on prophets, judges, and kings. Yet the overshadowing of God's power on a person is a unique expression. The meaning seems to be that God would cause a conception inside Mary. The manner of this conception is a mystery, and overly detailed speculation is unwise. The church has historically (and with great intellectual rigor) said this means Jesus is fully divine and fully human.

There is more than one sense in which Jesus is the Son of God, but the highest sense is literal: His Father, the One who caused Mary to conceive, was God. This still is not the highest realization about Jesus. Mary did not yet know that Jesus was the Son who had existed forever with God as God.

**God's creating power (Luke 1:36-37).** Gabriel explained the situation of Mary's relative, Elisabeth. Jesus' birth announcement in some ways parallels and exceeds everything great that has been said about John the Baptist. Some historians think the movement started by John the Baptist continued for a time into the early days of the church. It is possible that some of his disciples did not accept Jesus as the Messiah proclaimed by John. Perhaps Luke was careful to include the parallels and show the greater role of Jesus from the beginning in order to teach followers of John the Baptist faith.

Elisabeth was barren, and like many barren women in the Bible, she was enabled to conceive by divine intervention. Yet Mary's situation was more unimaginable. She conceived, without knowing a man, by the direct working of God. Elisabeth's son would be a prophet. Mary's son was the Son of God, human and divine. God the Creator has no limits and can make barren women—and one specially chosen virgin—conceive.

## MARY'S JOURNEY—Luke 1:38-40

**Accepting the calling (Luke 1:38).** Mary accepted her place as the domestic slave of God. Words for servanthood and slavery were interchangeable in the ancient world. To be a handmaid to a good master was to be a servant, blessed in many ways. Yet it did mean submitting to a higher authority. Mary could hardly have failed to realize that the role God demanded of her was difficult. She was being asked to bear the shame of reproach and even the danger of punishment for conceiving an ostensibly illegitimate child.

Mary's words of acceptance have been rightly viewed as remarkable. Though it may be difficult, even dangerous, a person of great faith and devotion will accept whatever God says is for the good. The benefits of God's redemption are too great to compare to our brief time of hardship. Faith like Mary's is a model for all who believe in the kingdom that never ends.

**Traveling to Elisabeth (Luke 1:39-40).** Assuming the home of Zacharias and Elisabeth was near Jerusalem, Mary's journey to Judea was about eighty miles. While still in the womb, John would signal his awareness of the greatness of the unborn child in Mary's womb. Two women, small in the eyes of the powerful, would offer psalms describing the goodness of God and the wisdom of His plan.

—*Derek Leman.*

# QUESTIONS

1. How do we know that Nazareth was regarded as unimportant?
2. Why was it important that Mary was unmarried and a virgin?
3. What is important about Joseph's descent from King David?
4. Why was Mary alarmed by Gabriel's blessing?
5. How was Mary favored by God?
6. How do descriptions of the child's greatness and His coming rule parallel a key passage about David?
7. What does God's power overshadowing Mary tell us about Christ's two natures?
8. What does the Bible mean when it refers to Jesus as the Son of God?
9. How was Elisabeth's conception similar to and yet different from Mary's?
10. How does Mary's response to Gabriel's message inspire people?

—*Derek Leman.*

## PRACTICAL POINTS

1. God is in control as He works out His plan of salvation for mankind (Luke 1:26-27).
2. As God had a plan for Mary, so He has a plan for us (vs. 28).
3. God deals with His people with grace and encouragement when they do not understand His workings (vss. 29-30).
4. God always fulfills His promises (Luke 1:31-33; cf. II Sam. 7:12-17).
5. Questioning God should strengthen the believer's faith, for the God of truth has the answers (Luke 1:34-37).
6. Obedience to the Lord is the key to God's blessings (vss. 38-40).

—Paul R. Bawden.

## RESEARCH AND DISCUSSION

1. What does it mean that Mary was espoused to Joseph (Luke 1:26-27)?
2. Why did the Angel Gabriel come to Mary? What does this tell us about Mary's relationship with God?
3. How would you feel if an angel appeared to you? Would you have the same feelings as Mary (vs. 29)?
4. How would Christ's birth fulfill Old Testament prophecy (Luke 1:31-33; cf. Isa. 9:6-7)?
5. Why was the Holy Spirit's coming upon Mary a miracle (Luke 1:35)?
6. Why do you think people deny this miracle today? If this miracle were not true, what would this mean for the possibility of salvation?
7. What does Luke 1:37 mean to you?

—Paul R. Bawden.

## Golden Text Illuminated

"Behold, thou shalt conceive in thy womb, and bring forth a son, and shalt call his name JESUS" (Luke 1:31).

This golden text was, of course, spoken by the Angel Gabriel to Mary, the mother of the Lord Jesus. It was spoken long before His birth. It was therefore a prophetic statement, a predictive prophecy, that foretold the sending of God's Son into the world. We should stand in awe of this text. In just a few words, we are reminded of God's awesome plan to send our Saviour into the world.

The angel made it clear in his prophetic words in this passage (Luke 1:31-33) that this sending would involve a wonderful and miraculous intervention. Mary would conceive a child while remaining a virgin. By His Spirit, God would miraculously work within her, and she would bring forth a child.

The name Jesus comes from a Hebrew word meaning "Yahweh saves." It speaks of God's salvation and our deliverance. So the name Jesus means "salvation," as Mary would certainly have recognized when the angel spoke this prophetic word to her. Matthew 1:21 makes this clear in another prophetic statement: "And she shall bring forth a son, and thou shalt call his name JESUS: for he shall save his people from their sins."

As we study the Old Testament concept of salvation, we see that it refers to that deliverance that moves us from distress to safety through divine power.

—Jeff VanGoethem.

LESSON 2                                    DECEMBER 8, 2013

# Scripture Lesson Text

**LUKE 1:46** And Ma'ry said, My soul doth magnify the Lord,

47 **And my spirit hath rejoiced in God my Saviour.**

48 For he hath regarded the low estate of his handmaiden: for, behold, from henceforth all generations shall call me blessed.

49 **For he that is mighty hath done to me great things; and holy *is* his name.**

50 And his mercy *is* on them that fear him from generation to generation.

51 **He hath shewed strength with his arm; he hath scattered the proud in the imagination of their hearts.**

52 He hath put down the mighty from *their* seats, and exalted them of low degree.

53 **He hath filled the hungry with good things; and the rich he hath sent empty away.**

54 He hath holpen his servant Is'ra-el, in remembrance of *his* mercy;

55 **As he spake to our fathers, to A'bra-ham, and to his seed for ever.**

56 And Ma'ry abode with her about three months, and returned to her own house.

# Mary's Song of Praise

## Lesson: Luke 1:46-56

Read: Luke 1:46-56

TIME: 7 or 6 B.C.     PLACE: hill country of Judea

GOLDEN TEXT—"Mary said, My soul doth magnify the Lord, and my spirit hath rejoiced in God my Saviour" (Luke 1:46-47).

## Lesson Exposition

**GRACE FOR MARY—Luke 1:46-49**

**Her praise of God (Luke 1:46-47).** Luke does not say that Mary's words were a prophetic utterance, but we might assume this is the case. When the Spirit came upon psalmists and prophets to declare His truths, they often repeated themes and phrases from earlier Scriptures. These were frequently in the form of poetry. Mary's psalm follows the patterns of Hebrew poetry, and it repeats many themes from the song of Hannah in I Samuel 2:1-10.

Mary is thought by most historians to have spoken Aramaic, which is very similar to Hebrew. Hebrew poetry exhibits correspondence of ideas rather than sounds—a feature known as parallelism. So we see ideas "rhyming" in Mary's psalm. Her soul magnified the Lord, and her spirit rejoiced in God her Saviour. To magnify the Lord is to describe His greatness in words, for our minds need words to express things greater than we are.

Mary's psalm alludes to the words of an earlier woman, Hannah, who was blessed with a miraculous birth as well. Hannah's child, coming to her after a long barrenness, would be a prophet and a priest.

**Her selection from among the lowly (Luke 1:48).** There are many ways in which Mary was from a low estate. She was young and lived in a small town. She was from a people dominated by Rome. She resided in the rural part of her nation, far from the center of power in Jerusalem. She may have been from a poor or somewhat poor family.

In her relationship to God she understood herself to be a handmaiden, a domestic slave serving the Master. Whatever He commanded, she must do. Yet the Master had not been hard on His handmaiden but had blessed her beyond all women. Mary knew that her exaltation from humble origins to being the mother of the Messiah would cause her name to be remembered forever, and she was overwhelmed by this awareness.

**Her appointment by the Mighty One (Luke 1:49).** "Great things" is a phrase used for acts of God that further the plan of redemption in history. In Deuteronomy 10:21, Moses spoke to the second generation from the Exodus, explaining that God had done "great and terrible things" in the deliverance from Egypt. Sometimes in the course of human history, God intervenes in large ways. Rescuing Israel from slavery was a "great thing," and so was the virginal conception of Messiah in the womb of Mary.

Mary understood the kingship of God and that He was moving history toward something purely good. It would fulfill all that we truly desire. God is the Mighty One, overcoming all powers of death and evil. His kingdom will be a time of complete victory over them. His name is holy because there is no other like it.

## GRACE FOR THE LOWLY—
Luke 1:50-53

**Showing mercy to God fearers (Luke 1:50).** The first two chapters of Luke's Gospel are, among other things, a chronicle of God-fearing Israelites of seemingly little importance. Zacharias and Elisabeth lived near Jerusalem and were blameless, keeping all the ordinances of the Law of Moses (vs. 6). Simeon lived in Jerusalem and waited fervently for the next great happening in God's plan to redeem Israel (2:25). He was just and devout. Anna the prophetess was in the temple courts every day, serving God with frequent fasting and prayer (vss. 36-37). Joseph and Mary were keepers of the Mosaic commandments, circumcising Jesus on the eighth day (vs. 21), making purification and sacrificing at the temple (vss. 22-24), and coming from Galilee to Jerusalem for the required feasts (vs. 41).

To fear God is to hold Him in reverence and be in awe of His splendor and greatness. This awe of God leads ordinary people to patient faith and eager expectation of good things from Him. Those who have this awe of God pass it down, generation to generation.

**Dethroning the proud (Luke 1:51-52).** Scot McKnight commented that the truths in Mary's psalm are most likely things Joseph and Mary would have taught Jesus as He grew up (*A Community Called Atonement,* Abingdon). In His earthly ministry, Jesus repeatedly stood up for the lowly and dethroned the proud with scathing denunciations of error and hypocrisy. The Bible repeatedly teaches that using power and domination for selfish interests is the way of evil. The way of justice, of God's goodness, is giving and healing rather than dominating.

Therefore, God's pattern of working in history includes bringing down the proud. The kingdom will be a reversal, so the first will be last (Luke 13:30). During this present evil age, self-importance and the brutal use of power work to gain certain things that people covet. God-fearing people do not covet these things. Whoever is proud will be humbled.

**Filling the hungry (Luke 1:53).** Jesus would grow up to speak about the hungry and how God would fill them (6:21). People can be hungry for food, hungry for justice, and hungry for God. Hunger is the acute awareness of absence, of a lack. God is a Shepherd, and those who know Him are never truly empty.

## GRACE FOR SERVANT ISRAEL—
Luke 1:54-56

**Helping servant Israel (Luke 1:54).** Mary's psalm is not merely about general principles involving all people. God's actions in history are specific, focused on bringing blessing to the whole world starting with one particular people, Israel. All of God's redeeming actions begin with and for Israel.

Mary understood and passed down to us in her psalm a vital truth of God. When Messiah was born to a virgin mother who was betrothed to an heir of David in the tribe of Judah from the people of Israel, the long-announced plans of God were finally coming to pass. God's grace to Mary is part of His plan of grace to Israel and, through Israel, to all people.

Although in the ultimate sense the Servant in Isaiah is Messiah Himself, this is because Messiah is the one person who fulfills all that Israel is supposed to be. The servant is Israel, as many verses in Isaiah declare (41:8; 42:19; 43:10; 44:1-2, 21, 26; 48:20; 49:3), with the greatest one in Israel being the only one who will complete what the Servant must do (49:5; 50:10; 52:13; 53:11).

**Remembering Abraham's seed (Luke 1:55).** The seed of Abraham means two different things. Both meanings involve promises of God that originated in the covenant He made with Abraham. First, the seed of Abraham is the people of Israel, the descendants of Abraham through his grandson Jacob (called Israel).

The second meaning of the seed of Abraham comes from the first meaning. One from the numerous seed, the whole people of Israel, would be the singular seed. Paul explained this in Galatians 3:16: "as of one, And to thy seed, which is Christ."

All the world is blessed through the seed of Abraham. This is true in both meanings. The people of Israel have brought the revelation of God through prophets, writings, and apostles to the world; the singular seed, Jesus, has brought untold riches.

Mary recognized that the promises made to Abraham two thousand years earlier were coming to pass. She had seen the angel. She had heard the word of God that she was to bear Messiah. Israel's long wait was nearing an end. Those who had kept faith through the long generations would at last see the next part of God's glorious plan. From the numerous seed of Abraham, God was bringing the singular seed.

**Returning home (Luke 1:56).** Mary had come when Elisabeth was six months pregnant (vs. 36). Now, as the two women chosen by God for such great things rejoiced together, Mary remained another three months.

Mary eventually journeyed back to Nazareth. Not many months later she would head south again, with Joseph, to Bethlehem, a little south of Jerusalem (Luke 2:4). The seemingly insignificant pilgrim, a God-fearing Israelite mother-to-be, knew what kings and generals could not know. The deliverance of Israel and the Gentiles was at hand. The promises to servant Israel (1:54) and Abraham's seed (vs. 55) were not for Israel alone. Under the eyes of Roman rule, a greater king than Caesar was about to be born.

—*Derek Leman.*

# QUESTIONS

1. What are ways Mary's psalm is like earlier biblical psalms?
2. God is infinite. In what sense are we able to magnify Him?
3. What are some ways that Mary might be considered lowly?
4. What does it mean to fear God?
5. How were the truths in Mary's psalm lived out in the words and deeds of Jesus?
6. How will the proud be brought down?
7. Why is the term "servant" applicable to both Messiah and Israel?
8. What are the two meanings of the seed of Abraham?
9. How did Mary's pregnancy relate to the promises?
10. How does the theme of bringing down the proud relate to Israel's leadership and also to Rome?

—*Derek Leman.*

## PRACTICAL POINTS

1. The believer should rejoice in the Lord (Luke 1:46-48; Phil. 4:4).
2. God's power, holiness, and mercy should cause us to give Him praise (Luke 1:49-50).
3. God should be praised for humbling the proud (vs. 51).
4. God exalts those who are weak (vs. 52).
5. Praise be to God for supplying the needs of His people (vs. 53)!
6. Riches can steal one's love for God.
7. God's prophetic Word is reliable (Luke 1:54-56; cf. Gen. 12:3).
—Paul R. Bawden.

## RESEARCH AND DISCUSSION

1. What does it mean for you to praise the Lord?
2. For what can you praise the Lord?
3. How might God's mercy be experienced from generation to generation (Luke 1:50)?
4. Why does God oppose the proud and the haughty (vs. 51)?
5. How does God supply your daily needs? What should your response be?
6. Why can riches be a stumbling block for accepting Christ as Saviour (vs. 53)?
7. How would the nation of Israel be affected by Christ's birth (cf. Zech. 9:9; Matt. 21:1-9)?
8. What relevance does Abraham have to the coming of Christ, the Messiah and the Son of God (cf. Gen. 12:1-3; Gal. 3:6-9, 28-29)?
—Paul R. Bawden.

## Golden Text Illuminated

"Mary said, My soul doth magnify the Lord, and my spirit hath rejoiced in God my Saviour" (Luke 1:46-47).

Mary was magnifying God because of what she had learned about her yet unborn child—He would be the long-expected Messiah, sent into the world by God. The song is Mary's grateful and thoughtful response to this news. It is a response of worship and praise.

It is doubtful that Mary simply made up the whole song on the spot. We see from the text that her words of worship and praise came from deep within her, from her soul and from her spirit. Being full of Scripture and full of God, her inner life was soaring. Much of the text of the song alludes to passages in the Old Testament.

Devout Jews of Mary's time often learned the Scriptures through memorization and recitation. Mary was likely steeped in Old Testament truth. What probably happened is that as Mary was at home in Nazareth and then as she traveled from her home to the hill country of Judah, she meditated upon Scripture, reflecting on what God was doing through her.

When her words came out, they were measured and thoughtful. She had begun to grasp the greatness of the promises that had been made to her by the angelic visitor. The Messiah was coming, and God had given her the privilege of bringing Him into the world! As a devout Jew, Mary no doubt knew of the long-expected Messiah and the biblical promises of His coming. That it was being fulfilled in her life was almost beyond comprehension.

—Jeff VanGoethem.

LESSON 3                                    DECEMBER 15, 2013

## Scripture Lesson Text

**LUKE 1:57** Now E-lis'a-beth's full time came that she should be delivered; and she brought forth a son.

**67 And his father Zach-a-ri'as was filled with the Ho'ly Ghost, and prophesied, saying,**

68 Blessed *be* the Lord God of Is'ra-el; for he hath visited and redeemed his people,

**69 And hath raised up an horn of salvation for us in the house of his servant Da'vid;**

70 As he spake by the mouth of his holy prophets, which have been since the world began:

**71 That we should be saved from our enemies, and from the hand of all that hate us;**

72 To perform the mercy *promised* to our fathers, and to remember his holy covenant;

**73 The oath which he sware to our father A'bra-ham,**

74 That he would grant unto us, that we being delivered out of the hand of our enemies might serve him without fear,

**75 In holiness and righteousness before him, all the days of our life.**

76 And thou, child, shalt be called the prophet of the Highest: for thou shalt go before the face of the Lord to prepare his ways;

**77 To give knowledge of salvation unto his people by the remission of their sins,**

78 Through the tender mercy of our God; whereby the dayspring from on high hath visited us,

**79 To give light to them that sit in darkness and *in* the shadow of death, to guide our feet into the way of peace.**

# Zacharias's Prophecy

## Lesson: Luke 1:57, 67-79

Read: Luke 1:57-80

TIME: 7 or 6 B.C.     PLACE: hill country of Judea

---

**GOLDEN TEXT**—"Thou, child, shalt be called the prophet of the Highest: for thou shalt go before the face of the Lord to prepare his ways; to give knowledge of salvation unto his people by the remission of their sins" (Luke 1:76-77).

---

## Lesson Exposition

The psalm of Zacharias is known as the Benedictus, from its first word in the Latin translation of Luke 1:68. By the Holy Spirit, Zacharias interpreted the birth of his son, John the Baptist, as heralding Messiah's coming.

**THE TIMES ARE UPON US—Luke 1:57, 67-69**

**The birth of John the Baptist (Luke 1:57).** Elisabeth and Mary had rejoiced together. The infant in the womb (to be named John) had leaped in recognition of his Lord in Mary's womb. The long-barren Elisabeth gave birth to her son. In keeping with custom, he would not be named until his eighth day of life (cf. vs. 59). In Genesis 17:12 and Leviticus 12:3 God commanded that circumcision for boys happen on the eighth day. The practice of naming the child on the eighth day (and not before) is evident in the New Testament both with John and Jesus (cf. Luke 2:21).

**The Spirit upon Zacharias (Luke 1:67).** Prior to the moment of his son's naming, Zacharias's ability to speak had been withheld by the power of God. While serving his priestly duties in the temple, Zacharias had been visited by the angel of the Lord inside the holy place of the temple. The angel had announced that Elisabeth would soon conceive, that the child would be named John, that John would be a Nazarite and full of the Spirit, and that he would advance the kingdom of God by his work (vss. 11-17). Zacharias did not believe at first (vs. 18), and thus God removed his ability to speak until that which had been foretold came to pass (vs. 20).

Zacharias delivered his psalm as prophecy. In biblical times the Spirit of the Lord came upon people for special empowerment. Some were empowered to do feats of strength (Judg. 14:6), or to muster and lead troops (6:34). Most often the Spirit came upon people to speak prophecy. Many prophecies in the Bible are in poetic form, like psalms, and much that is in the book of Psalms has prophetic significance.

**The visit of the Lord (Luke 1:68).** The first word from Zacharias's mouth was praise. In the language of prayer and public worship, what does it mean to speak of God as "blessed"? The idea is "May He be blessed by His people," as well as "He is surely blessed by His people." The one praying or worshipping recognizes something truly great and deserving of rejoicing in

Adult Bible Class

God's deeds and Person.

The idea of God visiting His people suggests a long period of divine silence (or near silence). Before John the Baptist, the last writing prophet had been Malachi. The history of Israel between the time of Ezra and that of John the Baptist had been a famine of prophecy. A similar use of the idea is found in Ruth 1:6, where Naomi heard that after a famine God "had visited his people," that is, returned rain and wheat to the land of Judah. Zacharias saw that the times were leading to a vital moment; the low whisper of God would soon be a shout.

**The raising of the horn (Luke 1:69).** The word "Messiah" means "anointed one" (signifying anointing with fragrant oil, a custom from biblical times). In I Samuel 2:10, the part of the prayer of Hannah alluded to in Luke 1:69, we read about "the horn of his anointed." The phrase is synonymous with "the horn of His king" (or, as applied to Jesus, "the horn of His Messiah").

In ancient poetry, the horn refers to the horn of a bull and signifies strength. One aspect of the character of Messiah is that He conquers evil and sets up the kingdom of God on earth (Dan. 2:44; 7:14). Our hope is in God's strength because the forces of evil appear so powerful to us.

## THE ANCIENT PROMISES ARE HERE—Luke 1:70-75

**The holy prophets (Luke 1:70-71).** Zacharias's son would be the first active prophet since Malachi.

What does it mean that the prophets have been around since the beginning of the world? Although it is possible that some thought of Adam as a prophet (he named the animals), it is more likely that the reference is to the Word of God. Psalm 33:6 says, "By the word of the Lord were the heavens made." Genesis 1 tells us that God created by His spoken Word. Also, the Spirit of God, the same Spirit who came upon Zacharias to speak this psalm and also upon all the prophets, was moving over the waters. Those who truly understand prophecy regard the creation of the world as an act of God's Word, just as the Bible is an act of His Word. The prophetic promises of salvation and deliverance from enemies go way back. They were never an afterthought.

**The covenant with Abraham (Luke 1:72-73).** The covenant with Abraham is larger in scope than the Mosaic covenant. Paul explained to his Gentile readers that they were included in the Abrahamic promise, which came prior to the Mosaic covenant with Israel (Gal. 3:15-17).

But even for Israel, the Abrahamic covenant is larger in scope. The Mosaic covenant promises blessings in agriculture, safety, and national strength for Israel. The Abrahamic promises are larger. They are unconditional. They include not only land and national existence but also multiplication, protection from curses (Gen. 12:3), and even the conquering of their enemies (22:17).

Zacharias, by the Spirit, revealed that his son would be part of bringing the next step in the unfolding move of God toward the messianic era.

**The holy community (Luke 1:74-75).** In the messianic era and in keeping with the promises to Abraham (Gen. 22:17), Israel would be delivered from all enemies.

The people who believe in such promises from God receive them actively. Not complacent about a free gift of God's power, real believers like Zacharias, Elisabeth, Simeon, and Anna served God fervently. A love relationship is mutual. Those among the people of God who understand faith also understand service, holiness, and good deeds as a way of life.

## THE FORERUNNER AND THE MESSIAH COME—Luke 1:76-79

**Knowledge and remission of sins (Luke 1:76-77).** The first century was a confusing time with many teachers. What the people needed was a prophet to bring into focus the teachings of the Scriptures.

But Israel's problem was not just ritual impurity, and Israel's solution was not just temple worship. They needed forgiveness and transformation.

Not only would John show Israel a new way of life—living as forgiven, purified people with a new devotion to good deeds—but he would also point to Messiah. Just as the waters of purification in the Torah made a person clean from ritual uncleanness, so Messiah would cleanse the conscience and make people fit to live with God. It would take more than water to remit sins. Thus, John would proclaim the Lamb of God, who takes away the sin of the world.

**The dayspring (Luke 1:78).** The image of the sun rising is fitting for the advancement of the messianic plan of God. The condition of life in this present age is darkness. Life is filled with gloom. Hovering over all the blessings, even in the best life under the sun, are the certainty of death, the reality of war, and the pains of illness and disability. The morning brings hope. Messiah is the "Sun of righteousness" who rises with "healing in his wings" (Mal. 4:2).

Zacharias's words here bring a similar message to the prologue in the Gospel of John. Messiah comes to give life, and this is the "light of men" (1:4). This light, Messiah's light, shines in the darkness and will not be overcome by the powers of evil and death (vs. 5). Verses 6-8 even associate the ministry of John with bearing witness to the light, just as Zacharias foretold that the birth of his son would herald the coming Light.

**The way of peace (Luke 1:79).** Zacharias revealed that the coming of God's promises is for the community of righteous believers—those who worship and live holy lives in expectation—as well as for those in darkness. He also revealed that the promise of light carries a responsibility. When the light shines, people of faith see better how to live. To know Messiah is to love the light. God is light. If we walk in the light, doing what His love shows us is truly good, we are in the true community of believers. The birth of John and Jesus meant a new passion for godliness.

—*Derek Leman.*

## QUESTIONS

1. Why did his parents wait until the eighth day to name John?
2. Why had Zacharias been unable to speak?
3. For what purpose did the Spirit fill Zacharias?
4. What does it mean that God visited His people?
5. What does the idea of a horn signify, and what does it have to do with Messiah (Son of David)?
6. What is implied by the statement that the speaking of the prophets goes back to the world's beginning?
7. How does the Abrahamic covenant relate to Israel being secure?
8. How was John to bring knowledge of the remission of sins?
9. What does the dayspring have to do with the coming of Messiah?
10. How does God's promise—His revealing light—cause His people to worship and serve more?

—*Derek Leman.*

## PRACTICAL POINTS

1. God's Word is totally reliable (Luke 1:57; cf. vs. 13).
2. God's redeeming grace should cause us to praise Him (vss. 67-68).
3. God miraculously used Old Testament prophets to speak His truth (vss. 69-70).
4. The eternal God keeps His Holy Word intact despite the passing of time (vss. 71-73).
5. God's Word brings the message of salvation to us (Luke 1:74-75; cf. Rom. 10:9-17).
6. God uses believers to be witnesses for Him of His forgiveness and grace (Luke 1:76-79).

—Paul R. Bawden.

## RESEARCH AND DISCUSSION

1. Who were the prophets, and what was the role of a prophet during biblical times?
2. How would Christ be a horn of salvation to the nation of Israel while providing deliverance from their enemies (Luke 1:69-71)?
3. Since Christ would fulfill the Abrahamic covenant, what does this tell us about the ways in which God keeps His Word (Luke 1:72-73; Heb. 6:13-20)?
4. What should Luke 1:74-75 mean to the follower of Christ?
5. What would be the supreme task of John the Baptist (cf. John 1:19-36)?
6. What message would John bring to God's people?
7. What does God's "tender mercy" mean in Luke 1:78?

—Paul R. Bawden.

## Golden Text Illuminated

"Thou, child, shalt be called the prophet of the Highest: for thou shalt go before the face of the Lord to prepare his ways; to give knowledge of salvation unto his people by the remission of their sins" (Luke 1:76-77).

Zacharias's prophecy came amid unique circumstances—those surrounding the birth of Jesus. Remember that Zacharias was struck mute when he did not accept the prophecy that he and his wife would have a child.

When Zacharias's tongue was finally loosened, what did he speak about? The subject of his prophecy was the messianic gift that was coming into the world. Our golden text concerns the unique role of Zacharias's son, John the Baptist, in this plan.

What was this role? First of all, Zacharias declared John's office. John the Baptist was to become a prophet of the Most High. He was given the task of speaking for God, as were all the prophets. John's unique role was to speak for God right on the threshold of the public ministry of the Lord Jesus—a very high privilege and sacred duty.

Then John's mission was outlined more specifically. He was to go before the Lord, preparing the way. John's ministry was to bear witness of Jesus and to prepare people for their own encounter with the Saviour.

Finally, Zacharias spoke of the content of John's message. It was to be a messianic message. The Lord Jesus would be all about granting salvation to sinners.

—Jeff VanGoethem.

LESSON 4                                    DECEMBER 22, 2013

# Scripture Lesson Text

**LUKE 2:1** And it came to pass in those days, that there went out a decree from Cae′sar Au-gus′tus, that all the world should be taxed.

**2** (*And* this taxing was first made when Cy-re′ni-us was governor of Syr′i-a.)

3 And all went to be taxed, every one into his own city.

**4 And Jo′seph also went up from Gal′i-lee, out of the city of Naz′a-reth, into Ju-dae′a, unto the city of Da′vid, which is called Beth′le-hem; (because he was of the house and lineage of Da′vid:)**

5 To be taxed with Ma′ry his espoused wife, being great with child.

**6 And so it was, that, while they were there, the days were accomplished that she should be delivered.**

7 And she brought forth her firstborn son, and wrapped him in swaddling clothes, and laid him in a manger; because there was no room for them in the inn.

**8 And there were in the same country shepherds abiding in the field, keeping watch over their flock by night.**

9 And, lo, the angel of the Lord came upon them, and the glory of the Lord shone round about them: and they were sore afraid.

**10 And the angel said unto them, Fear not: for, behold, I bring you good tidings of great joy, which shall be to all people.**

11 For unto you is born this day in the city of Da′vid a Saviour, which is Christ the Lord.

**12 And this *shall be* a sign unto you; Ye shall find the babe wrapped in swaddling clothes, lying in a manger.**

13 And suddenly there was with the angel a multitude of the heavenly host praising God, and saying,

**14 Glory to God in the highest, and on earth peace, good will toward men.**

15 And it came to pass, as the angels were gone away from them into heaven, the shepherds said one to another, Let us now go even unto Beth′le-hem, and see this thing which is come to pass, which the Lord hath made known unto us.

**16 And they came with haste, and found Ma′ry, and Jo′seph, and the babe lying in a manger.**

17 And when they had seen *it*, they made known abroad the saying which was told them concerning this child.

Adult Bible Class

# Jesus' Birth

(Christmas)

## Lesson: Luke 2:1-17

Read: Luke 2:1-20

TIME: 6 or 5 B.C.                    PLACES: Nazareth and Bethlehem

---

**GOLDEN TEXT**—"She brought forth her firstborn son, and wrapped him in swaddling clothes, and laid him in a manger; because there was no room for them in the inn" (Luke 2:7).

---

## Lesson Exposition

### JOURNEY—Luke 2:1-5

**The decree of Augustus (Luke 2:1).** Luke 2 brings the story of Jesus into the setting of the Roman Empire and the reign of Augustus, the first emperor and one revered as a god after his death. Paul, Luke's mentor and friend, taught in the congregations that Jesus is Lord. This is a way of saying that our Messiah is truly what Rome claimed its emperor to be: "Every tongue should confess that Jesus Christ is Lord, to the glory of God the Father" (Phil. 2:11).

Luke's Roman readers could not have missed the irony that Jesus was born during the reign of Augustus and in Bethlehem because of a decree of Augustus. An Italian archaeological find called the Priene Inscription tells us something of how Augustus was revered by later generations: "The birthday of the god has marked the beginning of the good news for the world" (Brown, *The Birth of Messiah*, Doubleday). Yet Luke's readers would see the real kingly birth. Augustus was nothing more than God's unwitting instrument.

**The census of Quirinius (Luke 2:2-3).** "Cyrenius" is a variant spelling of "Quirinius" (Publius Sulpicius Quirinius), the Roman governor of Syria. Joseph and Mary had to go to Bethlehem because of a decree of Caesar regarding a census. This is important because it explains why a family from Nazareth gave birth far to the south in Bethlehem.

**The journey of Joseph and Mary (Luke 2:4-5).** Leaving Nazareth in the north to journey approximately eighty miles south to Bethlehem is described as going "up" because Judah is mountainous. From any direction, going to Jerusalem is going up. Bethlehem, five miles south, is in the territory of Judah, called Judea.

Micah 5:2 says, "Thou, Bethlehem Ephratah, though thou be little among the thousands of Judah, yet out of thee shall he come forth unto me that is to be ruler in Israel; whose goings forth have been from of old, from everlasting." This city is apparently called Bethlehem Ephratah to distinguish it from Bethlehem of Zebulon (Josh. 19:15). The Messiah was to be born in the city of Messiah's precursor, King David.

## BIRTH—Luke 2:6-7

**Days accomplished for birth (Luke 2:6).** Does the idea of days being accomplished in Luke 2:6 mean simply that Mary's time of pregnancy was at an end? Or does it mean that Messiah was born at the time decreed by God? Both are true. Mary's term of pregnancy was indeed accomplished, but the words could be a hint of more. God brought history to just the right day for His birth.

**Swaddling and a manger (Luke 2:7).** When we read that there was no room at the inn, we should not picture a hotel or tavern with private rooms for single families. Bethlehem was a small town. Travelers might stay in homes. The added detail that there was no suitable lodging place for the birth of Jesus is necessary so that readers will understand why the infant Messiah was born in such a crude setting.

Swaddling clothes are strips of cloth or blanket wrapped around an infant to keep him secure. They are a sign of parental care. Swaddling was not a sign of poverty but of loving care. What is unusual is that a baby who was cared for by good parents would be laid in a manger, an animal feeding trough. This would be the definitive sign to the shepherds that they had found the correct baby.

## ANGELS—Luke 2:8-14

**Shepherds in the field (Luke 2:8).** The birth of Messiah happened in lowly circumstances. Shepherds have always been rather low on the social order. Certainly the announcement to shepherds was God's way of showing the humbleness of Jesus' birth. Yet there are specific reasons why shepherds were fitting witnesses of Messiah's birth. King David was a shepherd in Bethlehem. Ezekiel 34:23 promises Messiah would come as a shepherd. Jesus would use the shepherd illustration about Himself (John 10; cf. Matt. 26:31; Mark 6:34).

Perhaps there is one other reason shepherds made such an appropriate group of witnesses. Jesus Himself would be the Passover Lamb (John 1:29, 36; 19:33-37). He would be crucified on Passover. The shepherds of Bethlehem were the first witnesses to the birth of the Shepherd who was also the Lamb.

**The angel with a message (Luke 2:9-10).** Although "the angel of the Lord" appears a number of times in Scripture, he came only once to announce an accomplished birth: to shepherds concerning the birth of Jesus.

"Glory" in Scripture refers to the light of divine power, which the angelic beings bear as well, though it emanates from the Father. The same word can also be used for the glory of human kings. The humble shepherds saw heavenly, majestic light. Their fear was normal, even if they were merely seeing miraculous signs. Yet, more than this, the angelic messengers of God bear some of His holiness and splendor. Human beings are overwhelmed by even a small particle of God's glory.

"Good tidings" is a term especially related to Messiah and the kingdom of God. Isaiah 52:7 is the place where "good tidings" first develops the idea that God's rule will be established at a specific time through His Messiah. Our modern word "gospel" is derived from it. The four books about the life, death, and resurrection of Jesus have always been called Gospels. Paul said the gospel is the death, burial, resurrection, and appearances of Jesus (I Cor. 15:1-8). Jesus would tell the people the gospel of the coming kingdom (Luke 4:18; 7:22; 20:1).

"Good tidings" also relates the birth of Messiah to the kinds of things said about Roman emperors, especially Augustus. As mentioned previously, an ancient inscription found at Priene, Italy, calls the birthday of Augustus the "beginning of the good news for the world." Luke shows that the humble birth of Messiah, in contrast to the wealth of Augustus, was the true good tidings.

**The Saviour and a sign (Luke 2:11-12).** The angel of the Lord mentioned three titles for the infant: "Saviour," "Christ," and "Lord." Each of these titles had a different connotation.

God is many times called Israel's Saviour. A savior could be a human king sent to deliver in war (Isa. 19:20).

"Christ" means the same thing as "Messiah": one anointed, as in the ancient custom of anointing a priest or king. A major theme of the teaching of Jesus would be that the people did not yet understand the true mission of the Messiah.

Jesus was revealed to be more than a man and more than a human messiah figure. The word "Lord" used for Jesus in later contexts refers to His divinity. Yet the same word is also used of kings and high officials.

**The choir of angels (Luke 2:13-14).** The multitude of God's host (for He is the Lord of Hosts, that is, the heavenly armies) went far beyond other appearances of angels in the history of Israel.

Scripture indicates that the meaning of Jesus' birth is good news. The true glory is not that of the Roman emperor, with his legions and taxes, but the child born in a small Israelite town into the most humble of circumstances.

**RUMORS—Luke 2:15-17**

**The shepherds (Luke 2:15-16).** The shepherds found the scene just as the angel of the Lord had said (vs. 12).

**Spreading the news (Luke 2:17).** It was important for Luke's readers, living decades after Jesus, to know that the spreading of the good news of Jesus had been happening since the beginning. By their time, the tiny movement of Jesus followers in Jerusalem had spread all over the Roman Empire. The movement was still small, but no doubt all were amazed by how a small, originally Jewish group with a message about a Saviour (strange to Roman ears) could appear and grow in so many places.

The simple truth is that what has been revealed in Jesus is too wonderful to hide. Just as the shepherds told their story to many, so all followers of Jesus in every age have an understanding that other people would be blessed to hear.

—*Derek Leman.*

# QUESTIONS

1. Why was it important to Luke's first readers that Augustus decreed the census?
2. Why did God arrange for Jesus to be born in Bethlehem?
3. What two complementary meanings could "the days were accomplished" have in Luke 2:6?
4. Why is the mention that there was no lodging place for Joseph and Mary important?
5. What was the purpose of swaddling clothes?
6. Why were the shepherds fitting witnesses of Jesus' birth?
7. Why were the shepherds terrified by the angels?
8. What is important about the phrase "good tidings" (vs. 10)?
9. What is the meaning of the title "Christ," or "Messiah"?
10. Why did Luke write that shepherds spread the news about Jesus?

—*Derek Leman.*

## PRACTICAL POINTS

1. God acts in time with His eternal plan (Luke 2:1).
2. God uses even the acts of pagan leaders to fulfill His prophetic Word (vss. 2-3).
3. God uses obedient people to carry out His plan (vss. 4-6).
4. Christ's incarnation is a great miracle; God in the flesh identified with us (vs. 7).
5. God uses angels (messengers) to accomplish His eternal purposes on earth (Luke 2:8-14; cf. Heb. 1:13-14).
6. Our first response to God's calling should always be obedience (Luke 2:15-17).

—Paul R. Bawden.

## RESEARCH AND DISCUSSION

1. How do you think Joseph and Mary felt when they found out that there was no room for them in the Bethlehem inn?
2. What is the relationship between Luke 2:1-6 and Micah 5:2? What does a prophecy like this being fulfilled some seven hundred years later tell us about the accuracy of God's Word?
3. In what ways was the birth of Christ different from other births?
4. Why did God use angels to announce the birth of Christ (Luke 2:8-14; cf. Heb. 1:14)?
5. How might seeing the Christ Child have changed the lives of the shepherds? How might this compare to how Christ has changed your life?

—Paul R. Bawden.

## Golden Text Illuminated

"**She brought forth her firstborn son, and wrapped him in swaddling clothes, and laid him in a manger; because there was no room for them in the inn**" (Luke 2:7).

Think of how many people Joseph and Mary passed on their journey from Nazareth to Bethlehem! They no doubt passed right through Jerusalem. Surely, a lot of people saw them, but not many took note of them. When they got to Bethlehem, as our golden text points out, "there was no room for them in the inn." This often quoted verse displays the great irony of the Lord's entry into the world. The earthly origins of the Christian faith, the birth of Jesus, lay in the shadows of history.

Think about it. They had no doctors. There were no servants or workers to help. There was no money or wealth. No fame or headlines immediately emerged. Jesus was born in a simple way and embraced by His parents in the usual way of the ancient poor. He was simply swaddled and laid down in the most convenient place—in this case a manger, an animal's feed trough. It was all so very ordinary.

Let us not fall into forgetfulness. Let us celebrate the birth of Jesus. Let us go over the story again and again. Let us remember that He is the Saviour of the world. And let us proclaim this to a sleeping world so that perhaps God might awaken some afresh today.

Christ is called here the "firstborn." Elsewhere in God's Word He is called the firstborn of all those who will be saved and glorified (Rom. 8:29). May many more be born anew to salvation.

—Jeff VanGoethem.

LESSON 5                                    DECEMBER 29, 2013

## Scripture Lesson Text

**LUKE 2:25** And, behold, there was a man in Je-ru'sa-lem, whose name *was* Sim'e-on; and the same man *was* just and devout, waiting for the consolation of Is'ra-el: and the Ho'ly Ghost was upon him.

**26 And it was revealed unto him by the Ho'ly Ghost, that he should not see death, before he had seen the Lord's Christ.**

27 And he came by the Spir'it into the temple: and when the parents brought in the child Je'sus, to do for him after the custom of the law,

**28 Then took he him up in his arms, and blessed God, and said,**

29 Lord, now lettest thou thy servant depart in peace, according to thy word:

**30 For mine eyes have seen thy salvation,**

31 Which thou hast prepared before the face of all people;

**32 A light to lighten the Gen'-tiles, and the glory of thy people Is'ra-el.**

33 And Jo'seph and his mother marvelled at those things which were spoken of him.

**34 And Sim'e-on blessed them, and said unto Ma'ry his mother, Behold, this *child* is set for the fall and rising again of many in Is'ra-el; and for a sign which shall be spoken against;**

35 (Yea, a sword shall pierce through thy own soul also,) that the thoughts of many hearts may be revealed.

**36 And there was one An'na, a prophetess, the daughter of Pha-nu'el, of the tribe of A'ser: she was of a great age, and had lived with an husband seven years from her virginity;**

37 And she *was* a widow of about fourscore and four years, which departed not from the temple, but served *God* with fastings and prayers night and day.

**38 And she coming in that instant gave thanks likewise unto the Lord, and spake of him to all them that looked for redemption in Je-ru'sa-lem.**

# Jesus Presented in the Temple

Lesson: Luke 2:25-38

Read: Luke 2:21-40

TIME: 6 or 5 B.C.   PLACE: temple in Jerusalem

---

**GOLDEN TEXT**—"For mine eyes have seen thy salvation, which thou hast prepared before the face of all people" (Luke 2:30-31).

---

## Lesson Exposition

**SIMEON'S FAITH—Luke 2:25-28**

**His character and hope (Luke 2:25).** Jerusalem in Jesus' time was filled with people of various beliefs and affiliations. The power in Jerusalem was concentrated in the high priest and the chief priests, who were among the Sadducees. The city was home to adherents of various beliefs, including several groups of Pharisees, who believed in popular reform through devotion to the Mosaic ways of life. There were other groups here as well, including radical Essenes who felt the temple was too corrupt and who did not offer sacrifices.

In the midst of all these groups, whose identity and character have largely been lost to history, Luke's Gospel reveals another group in the city of God. There were individuals who do not seem to have been affiliated with the usual parties. Some of them shared a deep devotion to worshipping God at the temple as they waited for the promises of the messianic era to fall upon them. They were hopeful that Messiah would come in their own time.

Simeon is among those Luke revealed as the devoted faithful, along with Zacharias and Elisabeth, Anna, and, in a slightly different way (since they were from Galilee), Joseph and Mary. Like the Pharisees, they kept the ways commanded by Moses. Unlike the Pharisees and Essenes, they seem to have placed a greater emphasis on worship at the temple. Unlike the chief priests, they believed in supernatural promises.

**His divinely granted mission (Luke 2:26).** We see here that men and women who have the Spirit upon them may at times have knowledge of specific events in the future. The purpose of specific, individual revelations like this one to Simeon is not always for public proclamation. Luke did not say that Simeon was told to prophesy that the Messiah would appear in his lifetime. He merely said that God revealed this fact to Simeon personally.

**His divinely granted appointment (Luke 2:27-28).** On a particular day, Simeon came into the temple by the Spirit. Although the Spirit sometimes transported prophets supernaturally

Adult Bible Class

(Ezek. 3:14; Acts 8:39), the meaning here is more likely that the Spirit simply showed Simeon when to enter the temple and where to find Joseph, Mary, and the infant Messiah. This was a divinely revealed and granted appointment.

### SIMEON'S PSALM—Luke 2:29-32

**His satisfaction (Luke 2:29-30).** Having achieved the greatest purpose of his life, Simeon was ready to pass from this world into the next. For those who are near to God, there need be no fear about leaving this life; a better one is prepared for us. Simeon's testimony teaches us that while we live, it is good to seek the fullness of our purpose. Simeon's satisfaction and readiness to pass away have to do with being filled with meaning during this life. We should all seek rightness with God and people in preparation for death.

**His prophetic perception (Luke 2:31-32).** Though Jesus was only a small infant, Simeon knew that through Him God had prepared salvation. Salvation can mean all kinds of things, including the revival of Israel, rescue from oppression, realization of ancient promises, and, its ultimate meaning, reconciliation between God and human beings. Simeon knew this salvation had been prepared "before the face," or in the sight of, "all people." He likely meant that Messiah had come openly but was yet unrecognized. Messiah had come for all people, not just Israel.

Simeon related what he knew from Isaiah about the Servant who is a light to the Gentiles (Isa. 49:1-7). Almost no one in Israel in Simeon's time understood Messiah's role as Saviour of all people. Jewish literature from the time rarely connects the Servant in Isaiah with Messiah. Simeon already understood things about Jesus that the disciples would grasp only after the resurrection. Though Jesus would tell them His full mission, they would repeatedly not believe. Simeon, by the Spirit, saw far into the future and recognized the true identity of Messiah.

### SIMEON'S BLESSING—Luke 2:33-35

**Words of blessing and prophecy (Luke 2:33-34).** By this time the idea that their son was Saviour of Israel was not new to Joseph and Mary; what did amaze them was that there were those in Jerusalem who had been waiting for Him and recognized Him. The unfolding of the messianic promises was not an old story to them but the ongoing experience of their lives. To marvel at God's deeds is a kind of worship.

Why would Jesus be a sign—and furthermore a sign to be spoken against? He would be a sign that the messianic era had come. The blind would be healed. Repentance and faith in Israel would increase. Yet He would not fully bring the kingdom of God; so those who could not see God's purpose in Jesus would be scandalized by His claims and His death, and they would disbelieve reports of His resurrection.

**Words of warning (Luke 2:35).** The words of Simeon's prophecy to Mary are poignant. Her son would die by piercing. When she saw her son do things differently from what even she expected (cf. Mark 3:21, 31-35), when she saw Him rejected and was present at His crucifixion (cf. John 19:26-27), she would be pierced too.

### ANNA'S GOSPEL—Luke 2:36-38

**Her identity (Luke 2:36).** Other prophetesses in the Bible include Deborah (Judg. 4:4), Huldah (II Kings 22:14), and the daughters of Philip (Acts 21:8-9). Anna is one of a few women so designated in the Bible. Luke tells us she was married only seven years before being widowed. This is another indication of her devotion to

God, since she was widowed at a young age but chose not to remarry. This may imply that the mission she took up, described in Luke 2:37, started early in life after her husband died.

**Her character and mission (Luke 2:37).** Anna was eighty-four years old, having been a widow perhaps as long as fifty-five or more years. In ancient times, few people lived to be this old. Poor nutrition and the hardships of life claimed many at a young age.

The saying that Anna did not depart from the temple is best understood as a Jewish expression for frequent worship. We need not think she had an apartment in the temple precincts. Instead, Luke relates that she was known to worship and serve often and for long periods of time in the temple. She was a person of extra holiness who engaged in voluntary fasting and extended prayers for others. She went beyond mere obligation in these things. They were for her a special calling. Not everyone is able to devote his or her life to this kind of service.

**Her proclamation (Luke 2:38).** An extraordinary person like Anna understood the coming of Jesus into the world. She is part of a group we know about only from Luke—Jews not of the Pharisees, Essenes, or Sadducees who were especially devoted to waiting for the messianic promises to arrive. Since she was a prophetess, knowledge of how to find the Messiah most likely came the same way as for Simeon—by the Spirit.

Anna's thanks to the Lord could refer to a Jewish blessing, a psalm recitation, or to a new psalm given by the Spirit. Yet her words about Jesus were not limited to giving thanks. She also began telling others in the temple courts about seeing Him.

There must have been many others like Zacharias, Elisabeth, Joseph, Mary, Simeon, and Anna. These were an informal community—not a synagogue or a party in Judaism—of common Jews whose great hope was in the days when God would redeem Israel. They knew their nation was still in spiritual exile. They knew Rome was not Israel's greatest problem. It was a nation in need of faith and revival.

The promises of the messianic era included a new heart and spirit for Israel. The nation would be redeemed from its human past and its many failures. The crucial factor in revival was and is the presence of Messiah, the only Redeemer.

—*Derek Leman.*

# QUESTIONS

1. What sort of people in Israel are especially highlighted in Luke's Gospel?
2. What kind of faith and practice did these people emphasize?
3. What sort of knowledge did God give by the Spirit to Simeon?
4. What can we learn from Simeon's readiness to leave this world after seeing Messiah?
5. From what Scriptures did Simeon know that the Messiah would be a light to Gentiles?
6. How would Jesus' coming be a sign of what was in people's hearts?
7. Why did Simeon say that Mary's own soul would be pierced?
8. What women are designated as prophetesses in the Bible?
9. What did Anna do after giving thanks for seeing the infant Messiah?
10. Why did Israel in Anna's day need redemption?

—*Derek Leman.*

## PRACTICAL POINTS

1. The Holy Spirit gives the believer understanding regarding who Jesus is (Luke 2:25-26).
2. As Jesus was dedicated to God, so we should dedicate ourselves to Him (Luke 2:27-29; cf. Rom. 12:1-2).
3. Jesus Christ came to provide salvation for both the Gentiles and the Jews (Luke 2:30-32).
4. If Christ has revealed His light in your heart, spread that light to others.
5. Jesus affects people in different ways, revealing what is in their hearts (vss. 33-38).
6. Like Anna, we can thank the Lord for saving us and then go tell others that He has provided redemption for them as well.

—Paul R. Bawden.

## RESEARCH AND DISCUSSION

1. Simeon was "just and devout, waiting for the consolation of Israel" (Luke 2:25); Anna prayed and fasted and "looked for redemption" (vs. 38). How are you preparing for the Lord's second coming?
2. What can we learn about God from the fact that He had revealed to Simeon that he would see the Saviour in his lifetime?
3. What is the significance of the description of Jesus as a "light" to the Gentiles and the "glory" of Israel (vs. 32)?
4. Today we have the completed Word of God; how does God give insight into understanding His Word and applying it to our lives (cf. I Cor. 2:12-13)?

—Paul R. Bawden.

## Golden Text Illuminated

"For mine eyes have seen thy salvation, which thou hast prepared before the face of all people" (Luke 2:30-31).

The background of this golden text is the Old Testament law of the firstborn, as Luke 2:23-24 makes clear.

We do not have a lot of information about Simeon. We do not know who he was or what position he occupied in Hebrew society. This is the only passage in God's Word that mentions him. He seems to have been one of those faithful, devout, Bible-reading Israelites who longed for the coming of the Messiah. The Spirit of God spoke to Simeon about the sending of the Messiah into the world (Luke 2:26) and then graciously led him to the temple. The Lord was there at the same time.

It was then, having taken the infant Lord Jesus into his arms, that Simeon uttered the powerful words of Luke 2:30-31. He acknowledged that the Lord Jesus had been sent into the world for the purpose of salvation. He could see in the life of this little child a worldwide salvation based upon all the messianic promises of God's Word. He did not know the story as we know it now, with knowledge of the Cross and all the surrounding events. But by prophetic utterance he proclaimed that this child would bring salvation to the world.

We celebrate this blessing in our churches and families. Christ was sent into the world to save sinners, and His coming was marked by a beautiful ceremony of redemption as He was presented in the temple.

—Jeff VanGoethem.

LESSON 6                                    JANUARY 5, 2014

## Scripture Lesson Text

**LUKE 6:1 And it came to pass on the second sabbath after the first, that he went through the corn fields; and his disciples plucked the ears of corn, and did eat, rubbing** them **in** their **hands.**

**2 And certain of the Phar′i-sees said unto them, Why do ye that which is not lawful to do on the sabbath days?**

3 And Je′sus answering them said, Have ye not read so much as this, what Da′vid did, when himself was an hungred, and they which were with him;

**4 How he went into the house of God, and did take and eat the shewbread, and gave also to them that were with him; which it is not lawful to eat but for the priests alone?**

5 And he said unto them, That the Son of man is Lord also of the sabbath.

**6 And it came to pass also on another sabbath, that he entered into the synagogue and taught: and there was a man whose right hand was withered.**

7 And the scribes and Phar′i-sees watched him, whether he would heal on the sabbath day; that they might find an accusation against him.

**8 But he knew their thoughts, and said to the man which had the withered hand, Rise up, and stand forth in the midst. And he arose and stood forth.**

9 Then said Je′sus unto them, I will ask you one thing; Is it lawful on the sabbath days to do good, or to do evil? to save life, or to destroy it?

10 And looking round about upon them all, he said unto the man, Stretch forth thy hand. And he did so: and his hand was restored whole as the other.

11 And they were filled with madness; and communed one with another what they might do to Je′sus.

Adult Bible Class

# Honoring the Sabbath

## Lesson: Luke 6:1-11

Read: Luke 6:1-49

TIME: A.D. 28            PLACE: Galilee

**GOLDEN TEXT**—"Then said Jesus unto them, I will ask you one thing; Is it lawful on the sabbath days to do good, or to do evil? to save life, or to destroy it?" (Luke 6:9).

## Lesson Exposition

**LORD OF THE SABBATH—**
**Luke 6:1-5**

**Rubbing grain on the Sabbath (Luke 6:1).** On the Sabbath Jesus was passing through a grain field with His disciples. Presumably, He and the disciples had already attended the synagogue service and were walking in the afternoon or evening. This was probably a short walk, since Jesus appears to have observed the traditional understanding about limited travel on the Sabbath (cf. Matthew 24:20).

**Not lawful on the Sabbath (Luke 6:2).** The Pharisees were a fraternity of middle-class men whose common goals included an increased observance of commandments from the Bible. They were based in Jerusalem, not Galilee, and must have been following Jesus to evaluate whether He was a threat, a genuine teacher, or something else (Sanders, *Judaism: Practice and Belief*, Trinity Press International).

What the Pharisees objected to was the disciples picking grain on the Sabbath. By A.D. 200, the rabbis had clarified that thirty-nine types of work were not permitted on the Sabbath, including "reaping" (Mishnah Shabbat 7:2). As far as the beliefs of the Pharisees in the first century, the New Testament is our primary source. There are no rabbinic writings from earlier than the Mishnah in A.D. 200.

It is important to realize that neither Jesus nor His disciples violated basic laws like the Sabbath. The disputes between Jesus and the Pharisees over the Sabbath concerned additional rules about what was forbidden on the Sabbath. The rabbis themselves called the Sabbath rules they devised "mountains hanging by a hair" of evidence (Mishnah Hagigah 1:8).

Thus, the disputes Jesus had with the Pharisees on this matter do not concern overturning the Sabbath law of the Bible as a requirement for Jews. The Sabbath was and remains today a sign between God and the Jewish people (Exod. 31:13).

**A Sabbath riddle (Luke 6:3-4).** Jesus gave His critics a true riddle to ponder with the story from I Samuel 21:6 about David receiving the sacred bread from the tabernacle at Nob (cf. Exod. 25:30). The consecrated bread in the tabernacle was replaced every Sabbath, and it was to be eaten by the priests alone (Lev. 24:5-9). Yet David and his men ate the bread, and Ahimelech allowed it.

The event in David's life resembles what was happening with Jesus and the disciples. Jesus may be compared to David, the disciples to David's men, and the Pharisees to Doeg the Edomite and Saul's men who were pursuing David (cf. I Sam. 21:7). So it does seem that Jesus was claiming to have a moral and royal authority like David's. He and His disciples were doing God's work, as David had been, and He had the authority to authorize His disciples to pick grain in a field on the Sabbath. Jesus was using the David story as a sort of parable and illustration of His authority.

**A Sabbath principle (Luke 6:5).** There are two prevailing interpretations of this saying. It is possible that both interpretations are correct, since a teacher of Jesus' caliber can make profound statements that contain more than one truth at the same time. The first interpretation is that "Son of man" here refers to all people. In this interpretation, Jesus would be saying that people are more important than the Sabbath. Filling human needs like hunger should not be interfered with by any interpretation of Sabbath laws.

The second interpretation, which fits with the understanding of Jesus' use of the David story above, is that the Son of Man here is Jesus. He was claiming that He had a special authority to make rulings about what was permitted on the Sabbath.

This was a startling claim for Jesus to make to people who did not believe in Him. He expected full faith from these Pharisees. They should have been able to see that He truly was worthy of faith as the Lord of the Sabbath and even of the entire law of God.

## DOING GOOD ON THE SABBATH— Luke 6:6-11

**Two ways on the Sabbath (Luke 6:6-7).** The man was full grown and had a hand that had probably been disabled from birth. Jesus deliberately used the occasion of meeting this person not only to do a deed of lovingkindness but also to teach the Pharisees and the people watching what the Sabbath is really about.

Two ways of observing the Sabbath are on display in Luke 6:6-7. The way of Jesus is teaching and healing. In the synagogue He observed the Sabbath according to the customs of His people, focusing on the words of God in Scripture. He was also observing the Sabbath with the intention of doing good deeds.

The opposite way of observing the Sabbath is seen in the reactions of these Pharisees. They were probably in Galilee to observe and evaluate Jesus (since they likely were from Judea). They were apparently there to criticize. They would be caught by Jesus' words (Luke 6:9) and exposed as lacking true devotion to what the Sabbath is supposed to be about.

**A Sabbath question (Luke 6:8-9).** Because Jesus knew these men came to observe and criticize, He asked the man with the disabled hand to rise. While the man was standing, Jesus asked a question. Jesus used this occasion to teach something His disciples would never forget. It is a lesson about the meaning of the kingdom, of the people of God, and of the mission God has given Messiah and His disciples.

Jesus' question is not just about what is or is not permitted on the Sabbath. It is a question that penetrates to the very heart of God's will. Why did God give laws about a temple, Sabbaths, the ethics of love, and the requirement of studying and practicing what the Scriptures teach? True elements of religion, right from the Bible, can be practiced by those who love God and also by those who have no knowledge of God. A Jewish Sabbath or a Christian Sunday worship service is not automatically godly simply by virtue of being held on the "correct" day. What does God require on the Sabbath: good or evil?

These scribes and Pharisees planned evil—to accuse Jesus and get Him into some kind of trouble when He went down to Jerusalem. Jesus planned good—to teach and to heal a man with a disability. Jesus' lesson was pointed and simple: merely keeping the form of a command does not make one righteous. These scribes and Pharisees were in the synagogue on the Sabbath Day, but they were doing evil. A godly man or woman keeps the intent as well as the form of God's commands. It is good to obey a commandment like honoring the Sabbath or gathering with the church. Yet the wrong intent or the lack of desire to do what is right ruins even an act of obedience.

**Life and death on the Sabbath (Luke 6:10-11).** Many things in this world need to be restored. The Bible tells us what is broken in people and in creation. The world was subjected to God's curse, and it groans for wholeness (Rom. 8:20-22). Jesus came to do the work of God, to teach disciples what God is doing, and to start a movement of people with faith in Him as Messiah. Jesus is the Restorer of the broken world, and all things will be gathered together in Him (Eph. 1:10).

The question He had just asked (Is the Sabbath intended for good or evil?) was answered in the miraculous healing of the man in front of them. First, how could Jesus have divine power to heal unless He was doing God's will? Second, how could people have any doubt about the authority of His teaching when such a miracle demonstrated it?

By contrast, the scribes and Pharisees were untouched by the miracle. They were angry at being rightly condemned by His words. The miracle only added to their anger because they were so thoroughly proved wrong.

Jesus' teaching is not just about the Sabbath; it is about all of the commandments that are God's will. Jesus did the Father's work on the Father's day, and Jesus' disciples are to imitate Him.

—*Derek Leman.*

# QUESTIONS

1. What might lead us to believe that the walk through the grain field was a short one?
2. Why did the Pharisees think Jesus' disciples were breaking the Sabbath law?
3. Why is it important that Jesus did not violate any of God's actual Sabbath laws?
4. What was Jesus' point in citing the example of David and the tabernacle bread?
5. Who is the Lord of the Sabbath, and what does that mean?
6. How was Jesus keeping the Sabbath for the good while the scribes and Pharisees were keeping it for evil?
7. Why were the Pharisees in Galilee?
8. How did Jesus' question to the Pharisees get to the heart of the matter?
9. Why does having wrong motives ruin an act of obedience to God's commands?
10. How is Jesus' Sabbath restoration of what was broken a picture of what is to come?

—*Derek Leman.*

## PRACTICAL POINTS

1. God's people were required to provide food for the hungry; we should likewise care for the poor (Luke 6:1; cf. Deut. 23:25).
2. Self-righteous people are always enforcing rules that enable them to condemn others (Luke 6:2).
3. The spirit of the law leads us to praise God (Luke 6:3-4; cf. I Sam. 21:1-6).
4. Jesus is to be honored as Lord on the Sabbath—and on every other day (Luke 6:5).
5. We humans tend to look for opportunities to criticize other people (vss. 6-7)!
6. Believers in Jesus have many opportunities to honor Him by doing good—sometimes at great personal cost (vss. 8-11).

—Paul R. Bawden.

## RESEARCH AND DISCUSSION

1. What did the Pharisees accuse Jesus' disciples of doing (Luke 6:1)?
2. Why were the disciples not stealing when they plucked grain from another's field (cf. Deut. 23:25)?
3. Is it ever necessary to violate the letter of one law in order to obey the spirit of another (cf. I Sam. 21:1-6)?
4. What lesson did Jesus teach when He healed on the Sabbath?
5. What does Jesus' healing of the man's withered hand tell us about His Person and power?
6. What was Jesus telling the Pharisees about their traditions, and how does this apply to us?

—Paul R. Bawden.

## Golden Text Illuminated

**"Then said Jesus unto them, I will ask you one thing; Is it lawful on the sabbath days to do good, or to do evil? to save life, or to destroy it?" (Luke 6:9).**

According to Scripture, the main purpose of the Sabbath law was to devote a day wholly to God. Observing such a day was and is a part of honoring God's rule and reign over life. One day is to be set apart to foreshadow the eternal rest that awaits God's people.

The problem the Lord faced was that many of the religious Jews in His day had gone beyond the simple instructions of God's Word, adding many man-made Sabbath restrictions. Hence, the Pharisees objected to the Lord and His disciples feeding themselves from the fields on the Sabbath (Luke 6:1); they saw this as unlawful work. The Lord also healed a man with a withered hand (vss. 6-10), and they saw this as a violation of the Sabbath as well (vs. 11).

The Lord's opponents became enraged when He decided to heal the man. It is clear that they were missing the larger point of the Sabbath. The point the Lord was making to them was that He and His disciples were serving God in doing what they did. That fulfilled the purpose of the Sabbath!

Others develop all sorts of rules that obscure the true purpose of the Sabbath Day. Jesus' point was that we are allowed to do good on the Sabbath! The Sabbath is part of God's loving rule and reign over our lives. Let us welcome with joy the opportunity to properly give God His day!

—Jeff VanGoethem.

Adult Bible Class

LESSON 7                              JANUARY 12, 2014

## Scripture Lesson Text

**LUKE 6:20** And he lifted up his eyes on his disciples, and said, Blessed *be ye* poor: for yours is the kingdom of God.

**21 Blessed *are ye* that hunger now: for ye shall be filled. Blessed *are ye* that weep now: for ye shall laugh.**

22 Blessed are ye, when men shall hate you, and when they shall separate you *from their company,* and shall reproach *you,* and cast out your name as evil, for the Son of man's sake.

**23 Rejoice ye in that day, and leap for joy: for, behold, your reward *is* great in heaven: for in the like manner did their fathers unto the prophets.**

24 But woe unto you that are rich! for ye have received your consolation.

**25 Woe unto you that are full! for ye shall hunger. Woe unto you that laugh now! for ye shall mourn and weep.**

26 Woe unto you, when all men shall speak well of you! for so did their fathers to the false prophets.

**27 But I say unto you which hear, Love your enemies, do good to them which hate you,**

28 Bless them that curse you, and pray for them which despitefully use you.

**29 And unto him that smiteth thee on the *one* cheek offer also the other; and him that taketh away thy cloke forbid not *to take thy* coat also.**

30 Give to every man that asketh of thee; and of him that taketh away thy goods ask *them* not again.

**31 And as ye would that men should do to you, do ye also to them likewise.**

# Living as God's People

## Lesson: Luke 6:20-31

Read: Luke 6:17-36

TIME: A.D. 28   PLACE: probably a plateau near Capernaum

**GOLDEN TEXT**—"But I say unto you which hear, Love your enemies, do good to them which hate you" (Luke 6:27).

## Lesson Exposition

In Luke 6:20-31, Jesus' teaching focuses on blessings and woes as well as the way of love. The first and central message of Jesus was the kingdom of God. Both the Sermon on the Plain and the Sermon on the Mount strongly focus on living today in light of our faith in the coming kingdom.

### BEATITUDES—Luke 6:20-23

**Reversal for the poor (Luke 6:20).** Luke did not simply repeat the sayings found in the Sermon on the Mount. The sayings recorded here were given at a different time. They were delivered from a level place, and Luke 6:17-49 is often referred to as the Sermon on the Plain. To think properly about Jesus as a Jewish teacher with a band of disciples and crowds of curious onlookers, we should realize He gave His important sayings in numerous locations and occasions.

Luke 6:20, like other beatitudes of Jesus, wraps several truths in one. It embodies the reverse of common thinking, an antithesis to the idea that wealth is blessing. It portrays the sad reality of the present time, when people suffer poverty. It is a statement about the future, since the future time of God's kingdom is what will overtake the present suffering of poverty with happiness greater than any suffering.

**Reversal for the hungry (Luke 6:21).** In the future, God will bless the world with abundance. Those who plow for a new crop will meet with people still harvesting the bounty of food (Amos 9:13). God will make "unto all people a feast of fat things" and even "of wines on the lees well refined" (Isa. 25:6). Everyone will have enough, and the fare in the kingdom will be that of a wealthy person's table for all to enjoy.

**Reversal for the persecuted (Luke 6:22).** The experience of being ostracized, of having one's name cursed and reproached, is something literal that happened to Jesus' own disciples not long after His ascension. In the early days of the Jesus movement, Jewish disciples all over the Roman Empire found themselves literally ejected from synagogues. Non-Jewish disciples faced rejection by local authorities under Roman rule. It is important for someone reading Jesus' words today to understand that the persecution He was speaking of was as literal as hunger and poverty are literal.

Adult Bible Class

**Example of the prophets (Luke 6:23).** To those sitting on the plain of Galilee listening to His words, Jesus made the beatitude clear with the example of prophets like Isaiah and Jeremiah. As people in Jesus' time realized more and more what He was claiming to be, they would find themselves in danger if they believed. Jesus' message was more than ethical teaching. It was also about His identity as the One who came from heaven, the Messiah—and, more than that, the divine Messiah. Believing that message would put people at odds with Jewish authorities in Jerusalem and also with Rome.

The message of Jesus was dangerous. Disciples would be persecuted. Yet Jesus' generation respected the prophets of old, who opposed the powerful and were in some cases killed for their faithfulness to God.

## WOES—Luke 6:24-26

**Reversal for the rich (Luke 6:24).** Just as the beatitudes are reversals, so too are the woes. If the poor can look to the coming kingdom of God with hope, the rich ought to look ahead with concern. The reason for this is a theme repeated by the prophets as well as in the teaching of Jesus. The mere fact of having plenty is not the spiritual danger but rather the tendencies that go along with financial comfort. This teaching has deep roots in the Bible, in Scriptures that should have been well-known in Jesus' time.

When there are plenty of crops in the field, Moses had warned, do not forget God (Deut. 8:13-14). The psalmist wrote, "If riches increase, set not your heart upon them" (Ps. 62:10). In a parable, Jesus explained the problem with riches: we tend to be poor toward God when we are rich in the possessions that give ease in this life (Luke 12:13-21).

**Reversal for the satiated (Luke 6:25).** Jesus often ate with disciples and was accused of being a glutton (7:34). His warning is not against the act of eating, rejoicing, and having good conversation with friends and family. As with the previous woe on riches, the problem is the tendency of those whose wants are fully met to forget the Provider. Nearness to God in the heart is so valuable that some physical hunger is better than spiritual emptiness. In the same way, those who engage in superficial gaiety (or possibly laugh at the expense of others) will weep for eternity.

**Reversal for the respected (Luke 6:26).** The final woe is for those who take pride in position and esteem. The four woes are the obverse side of the four beatitudes. The poor and hungry can find blessing in the kingdom, while the rich and full should remember God and accept greater responsibility.

Society's esteem is not really a worthy goal to aim for. When pride of position dominates, we flatter and compromise. To keep our advantage, we politick and self-promote. It is all emptiness and folly. Flattery is putting out a trap for others (Prov. 29:5). A gentle rebuke in love does more for a friend (28:23).

## LOVE—Luke 6:27-31

**The extent of love (Luke 6:27).** It is not enough, Jesus said, to refrain from vengeance. The highest calling is to act in kindness toward our haters. Jesus' command to love our enemies means action, not emotion. This can be seen in the second half of Luke 6:27: "do good to them which hate you." Those who harm others oppose God's kingdom. If we truly love as God does and bring good into relationships—when we show kindness to the hateful—there is a possibility of repentance. There is hope that enemies will become friends. Our good deed may counteract evil.

**The spirit of love (Luke 6:28).** The world is full of insults and curses. Jesus' way is not to return them but to find a way to speak kindness in return for curse. If we do this insincerely, people usually see through our hypocrisy. But if we grow nearer to God so that we love people as He does, we can truly wish the best for people who are rude and unkind.

More serious are those who spitefully use us. We may come to harm because of their actions. Instead of returning vengeance or bitterness, we must learn to have so much love that we pray sincerely for their betterment. To consistently have this kind of love is a hard thing to attain.

**The practice of love (Luke 6:29).** This is not about becoming a willing victim of serious violence. It is not spiritual to be injured. Jesus taught His disciples to flee from danger (cf. 21:21).

This should be interpreted as not being so attached to possessions. People are not obligated to let all thieves take until they can barely survive. Yet in many cases our objection to insults and loss is not about what we truly need. If we grow in faith far enough, even our pride and possessions will not own us—God alone will.

**The extent of generosity (Luke 6:30).** As is the case with all of Jesus' teaching on loving completely, we could take the teaching too far. The apostles did teach reasonable limits on giving. Consider Paul's limits on who should receive widows' support from the congregation (I Tim. 5:3-16).

Nonetheless, the extent of generosity God requires is a willingness to give to whoever asks. This does not mean we must fill every need presented to us, but we can usually give something.

**The definition of active love (Luke 6:31).** God had taught Israel long before, "Love thy neighbour as thyself" (Lev. 19:18). Hillel the Great, the rabbi who died about forty years before the ministry of Jesus, famously interpreted this to mean we should not do to others what we do not want done to us. Jesus viewed it from the positive side: to love as we love ourselves means to do for others what we would want done for us.

We want encouragement, help when in need, friendship, and protection. In general we want to be loved and treated fairly. In the coming kingdom of God, all needs will be met. Everyone will be loved. So in this present time, those of us who follow the King and believe in the kingdom should love in such a way as to make the future perfection a closer reality.

—Derek Leman.

# QUESTIONS

1. What accounts for the differences in wording between similar passages in Matthew and Luke?
2. What hope does the promise of the kingdom hold for the hungry?
3. How was Jesus' promise of blessing for the persecuted especially pertinent to His disciples and early Christians?
4. How did Jesus' teaching go beyond mere ethical teaching?
5. What made believing Jesus' message dangerous?
6. What are the real spiritual dangers associated with wealth?
7. What has no place in God's kingdom?
8. How do we know that Jesus meant the actions of love more than the emotions?
9. To what extent does God require generosity from us?
10. What does the way of love have to do with the kingdom?

—Derek Leman.

## PRACTICAL POINTS

1. Recognizing spiritual poverty is a must in order to experience God's eternal riches in Christ (Luke 6:20).
2. To hunger after God should be our first desire (vs. 21).
3. True sorrow can lead to God's joy (cf. II Cor. 7:10).
4. God rewards suffering for Him, bringing His joy to those afflicted (Luke 6:22-23).
5. Trusting in wealth, pleasure, or fame brings only death (vss. 24-26).
6. Be Christlike to those who are your enemies (vss. 27-30).
7. Enjoy living for the Lord in His power (vs. 31).

—Paul R. Bawden.

## RESEARCH AND DISCUSSION

1. What does Jesus' healing ministry tell us about how He saw people and identified with them (cf. Luke 6:17-19)?
2. What are the four blessings that Jesus gave and their rewards? Why is such teaching so foreign to our thinking?
3. How might the four woes apply to our lives today?
4. How can you love your enemies and do good to those who hate you?
5. Have you ever had someone curse you because of Christ?
6. What is the primary effect of praying for those who mistreat you?
7. What does it mean for believers to love unconditionally?
8. What enables us to be Christlike toward people (cf. Gal. 5:22-25)?

—Paul R. Bawden.

## Golden Text Illuminated

**"But I say unto you which hear, Love your enemies, do good to them which hate you" (Luke 6:27).**

Jesus said we are to practice love toward our enemies. This is a powerful ethical demand for those who want to live for God in this world. It certainly is not easy to carry out. It goes against fallen human nature. It can offend our sense of justice and fair play. But this is what the Lord asks of us.

Let us consider the meaning of "love." Love should not be thought of only as an emotion. We may not have good feelings toward those who have wronged us or slandered us or opposed us for no good reason. But the Lord is not asking us to have warm feelings toward them. He is asking us to love them. Love in this context refers to an unconditional willingness to do good to those who may be our enemies.

How do our enemies view us? Do they see something different at work in our lives? This is what the Lord is asking of us. This is what He rewards. This is what advances His name, rule, and kingdom.

So loving our enemies is not primarily designed to offer a pragmatic solution for our troubled relationships, although it may be helpful in that regard. It is meant to give evidence of the presence of God in our lives and to advance His name and kingdom. We are to deal with others as God has dealt with us—in love and mercy. It is vital that we live differently as God's people in the world. This is what testifies of the reign and kingdom of God in the midst of the world.

—Jeff VanGoethem.

LESSON 8                                    JANUARY 19, 2014

## Scripture Lesson Text

**LUKE 14:7** And he put forth a parable to those which were bidden, when he marked how they chose out the chief rooms; saying unto them,

8 **When thou art bidden of any *man* to a wedding, sit not down in the highest room; lest a more honourable man than thou be bidden of him;**

9 And he that bade thee and him come and say to thee, Give this man place; and thou begin with shame to take the lowest room.

10 **But when thou art bidden, go and sit down in the lowest room; that when he that bade thee cometh, he may say unto thee, Friend, go up higher: then shalt thou have worship in the** presence of them that sit at meat with thee.

11 For whosoever exalteth himself shall be abased; and he that humbleth himself shall be exalted.

12 **Then said he also to him that bade him, When thou makest a dinner or a supper, call not thy friends, nor thy brethren, neither thy kinsmen, nor *thy* rich neighbours; lest they also bid thee again, and a recompence be made thee.**

13 But when thou makest a feast, call the poor, the maimed, the lame, the blind:

14 **And thou shalt be blessed; for they cannot recompense thee: for thou shalt be recompensed at the resurrection of the just.**

Adult Bible Class                                      39

# Showing Humility

Lesson: Luke 14:7-14

Read: Luke 14:7-24

TIME: A.D. 30            PLACE: probably in Perea

**GOLDEN TEXT**—"Whosoever exalteth himself shall be abased; and he that humbleth himself shall be exalted" (Luke 14:11).

## Lesson Exposition

**LIVING FOR GOD'S EXALTATION—Luke 14:7-11**

**A parable on self-glorification (Luke 14:7).** The rabbis, who became the authorities in Judaism, were not fully developed as a movement in Jesus' time. Nonetheless, small circles of teachers with disciples had already been meeting and discussing Scripture, doctrine, and how to practice the commandments a few generations before Jesus.

The primary purpose of a parable was to use praise and blame to motivate change (Stern, *Parables in Midrash,* Harvard University Press). Parables also communicated higher truths, beliefs about God that should affect behavior. This is exactly what Jesus did in the incident in this week's study. He berated a group of Pharisees when He witnessed their behavior at a gathering of rabbis.

**The descent of the self-glorified (Luke 14:8-9).** The Pharisees sought the best places at the table. "Rooms" may mean both places at the table and also a choice of several rooms in the house. Jesus observed this behavior and noted that it went against a heavenly truth.

In Jesus' parable this dinner is compared to a wedding feast. A wedding was the most important social occasion and one in which a house would be filled to overflowing with guests. Further, a wedding in many parables suggests God as the father and Messiah as the groom. This parable of Jesus hinted at the idea of one's status before God in life, both on earth and in heaven.

Those who glorify themselves invite the master of the banquet to humble them. The problem with presuming a place before God is that He is the Judge and we are not. When we think more of ourselves than is proper, we subject ourselves to being put down.

**The ascent of the God-exalted (Luke 14:10).** It is better to assume a low position. Accepting a low place invites the host to notice us and offer us a better one.

Given that the wedding parables often use the host to represent God, the principle Jesus was teaching had to do with more than social etiquette. The highest place in God's eyes is that of a servant (Mark 10:43).

**The glorification from God (Luke 14:11).** Truly good parables point to heavenly truths. The basic principle of exaltation by God was nothing new. God had revealed it long before, espe-

40

cially in the inspired wisdom literature of the Bible.

This truth reflects God's character and will. Jesus' parable cast blame on the Pharisees, whose actions suggested a low view of God. His parable shows that the way to attain praise is to be the humble type of person God would exalt.

## LIVING FOR THE RESURRECTION—Luke 14:12-14

**Advice about earthly gain (Luke 14:12).** The advice Jesus gives here is related to the parable He told in four ways. First, it was given on the same occasion and was based on the same event. Second, it features the same general topic of reward and glorification in the life to come. Third, it also relates to a dinner or banquet. Finally, the advice concerns the coming resurrection, which is a part of that glorification by God that Jesus spoke about in verses 10-11. Yet this advice is also different from the parable. Whereas the parable was about the guests seeking honor, the advice was that the host seek reward from God in the judgment.

Although the advice to the host does literally apply to hospitality and reward from God for selflessly welcoming disadvantaged people, it is also about more. The topic includes wisdom and prophetic principles of recompense in this life and the next.

Jesus did not literally mean there is something wrong with inviting friends and family for dinner. But giving hospitality often includes an expectation of a return invitation in the future.

**Divinely protected ones (Luke 14:13).** The ones on Jesus' invitation list are the same ones protected by God in the laws He gave to Israel. Prophecy said Messiah would come to heal the lame, blind, and deaf. He would give good news to the poor and provide help for the maimed (Isa. 35:5-6; 61:1; cf. 56:3).

**Reward at the resurrection (Luke 14:14).** The parable was about seeking God's exaltation through service and humility rather than glorifying ourselves. The advice to the host is about offering kindness to those who cannot return it so that we will receive kindness from God. To care for the poor is to provide a loan to God that God Himself will repay (Prov. 19:17).

In the life to come, the righteous and humble will always be exalted.

The final resurrection will be of the just, of those justified by God's declaration. The Pharisees who heard Jesus believed this, but their behavior was not measuring up to their alleged beliefs.

—*Derek Leman.*

# QUESTIONS

1. How long had the rabbinical movement been developing in Jesus' day?
2. What was the primary purpose of a parable?
3. Why did Jesus address the Pharisees?
4. How did wedding parables generally symbolize God and His relationships with people?
5. What does the place we assume at a gathering have to do with our faith in God's reward?
6. What do good parables point to?
7. How is Jesus' advice to the host like the parable?
8. How is Jesus' advice different from the parable?
9. What are several reasons kindness toward the needy brings a divine reward?
10. What is the resurrection of the just, and why was it a choice topic?

—*Derek Leman.*

# PRACTICAL POINTS

1. Never seek to take glory for yourself (Luke 14:7-8).
2. Pride comes before a fall (vs. 9).
3. Let another person give you honor, not yourself (vs. 10).
4. Selfishness always leads to pride and division, whereas selflessness leads to harmony in relationships (vs. 11).
5. Invest your life not in those who are able to return the favor but in those who are not able to pay you back (vss. 12-13).
6. God rewards humility and Christlike service (vs. 14).

—Paul R. Bawden.

# RESEARCH AND DISCUSSION

1. How might people today take selfish advantage of another person's invitation to an event?
2. What should your attitude be when you are asked to be part of a family, church, or civic event?
3. What is the ultimate example of true humility in life (cf. Phil. 2:5-11)?
4. What does it mean to possess Christ's obedient mind as a follower of Him (cf. I Cor. 2:16), and how do you put it to work?
5. What is involved in putting others first without expecting to receive anything in return?
6. Why is the Lord's humility so different from our humility?
7. Is it wrong to anticipate rewards at the final judgment?

—Paul R. Bawden.

# Golden Text Illuminated

"Whosoever exalteth himself shall be abased; and he that humbleth himself shall be exalted" (Luke 14:11).

The background of this golden text is a parable the Lord told about seeking the best places to sit at a wedding feast (Luke 14:7-10). The instruction of the parable is to seek the lesser places to sit, lest a person be humiliated by being asked to move. It is tempting to want to have the higher, more prominent place to sit, but this is not wise; nor is it the Lord's way for His people.

The golden text then frankly admonishes us to not exalt ourselves by seeking a prominent position or by trying to associate with those who are prominent. The warning is that if we do so, we might find ourselves "abased." To be abased is to be brought low, to be put into a humbling situation. God has a way of teaching us to be humble.

We should willingly humble ourselves at the outset rather than wait for God to do something to bring us to the place of humility. The promise is that if we do so, God will exalt us. In order to go up, we must go down. If we go down, we will go up. If we put ourselves up, God will bring us down. This simple teaching is profoundly challenging to fallen human nature.

How do we fulfill such a demanding ethic? The secret of this is to put ourselves under the rule and dominion of God. If our lives are surrendered to His glory, we become increasingly unconcerned with our own glory. We will accept being humbled or exalted, whatever the Lord wants.

—Jeff VanGoethem.

LESSON 9　　　　　　　　　　　　　　　　　　　　JANUARY 26, 2014

## Scripture Lesson Text

**LUKE 16:19** There was a certain rich man, which was clothed in purple and fine linen, and fared sumptuously every day:

**20 And there was a certain beggar named Laz'a-rus, which was laid at his gate, full of sores,**

21 And desiring to be fed with the crumbs which fell from the rich man's table: moreover the dogs came and licked his sores.

**22 And it came to pass, that the beggar died, and was carried by the angels into A'bra-ham's bosom: the rich man also died, and was buried;**

23 And in hell he lift up his eyes, being in torments, and seeth A'bra-ham afar off, and Laz'a-rus in his bosom.

**24 And he cried and said, Father A'bra-ham, have mercy on me, and send Laz'a-rus, that he may dip the tip of his finger in water, and cool my tongue; for I am tormented in this flame.**

25 But A'bra-ham said, Son, remember that thou in thy lifetime receivedst thy good things, and likewise Laz'a-rus evil things: but now he is comforted, and thou art tormented.

**26 And beside all this, between us and you there is a great gulf fixed: so that they which would pass from hence to you cannot; neither can they pass to us, that *would come* from thence.**

27 Then he said, I pray thee therefore, father, that thou wouldest send him to my father's house:

**28 For I have five brethren; that he may testify unto them, lest they also come into this place of torment.**

29 A'bra-ham saith unto him, They have Mo'ses and the prophets; let them hear them.

**30 And he said, Nay, father A'bra-ham: but if one went unto them from the dead, they will repent.**

31 And he said unto him, If they hear not Mo'ses and the prophets, neither will they be persuaded, though one rose from the dead.

# Instruction on True Wealth

## Lesson: Luke 16:19-31

Read: Luke 16:1-31

TIME: A.D. 30  PLACE: probably in Perea

---

**GOLDEN TEXT**—"If they hear not Moses and the prophets, neither will they be persuaded, though one rose from the dead" (Luke 16:31).

---

# Lesson Exposition

### A CONTRAST IN PRESENT FORTUNES—Luke 16:19-21

**The unnamed rich man (Luke 16:19).** Some have doubted that this story is a parable. The fact that one of the characters in the story is named has convinced some that Jesus was relating true events on earth and in the abode of the dead. The very context of this story of the rich man and Lazarus suggests it is a parable. The early rabbis used parables to persuade their hearers.

Certain Pharisees were mocking Jesus. These men were lovers of money. They professed true belief in God and claimed that His commandments were central in their lives. Yet they were selfish rather than generous when it came to money.

Therefore, Jesus began His parable with a rich man who illustrated the attitude of these Pharisees. The description of his clothing as purple evokes kings' apparel, as in Judges 8:26. The rich man's dining habits involved daily banquets.

**The poor man, Lazarus (Luke 16:20-21).** It is crucial to the story that Lazarus was at the gates of the rich man, thus casting blame on the rich man for not keeping the positive commandments of the Law.

### A CONTRAST IN FUTURE FORTUNES—Luke 16:22-24

**Two different fortunes (Luke 16:22-23).** Why did Lazarus merit such blessed treatment by angels after death? Jesus did not say. Lazarus was borne by angels to the bosom of Abraham. At a formal Jewish meal, the guests reclined on lounges around a low table. To be in someone's bosom means to be next to him, so that one's head is near his chest. Lazarus had been brought to the table of Abraham (cf. Matt. 8:11; Luke 13:28). Abraham had received the great promise of a covenant in which all peoples could find blessing from God. Feasting at his table in the afterlife pictures the ultimate blessing of God. Meanwhile, the rich man was being tormented in hell.

**The rich man's bitter reversal (Luke 16:24).** The key irony in this reversal is that the rich man had not even given crumbs to Lazarus before. Now he wanted Abraham to send Lazarus to give him mere drops of water. Comparing crumbs to drops, the rich man could now see the error of his former ways.

Verses like this one tell us something about judgment in the afterlife. While some Christians are uneasy with the traditional view of hell, it is essential that we acknowledge all the specifics provided in Scripture.

## PRINCIPLES OF REWARD AND JUDGMENT—Luke 16:25-26

**The principle of reversal (Luke 16:25).** The principle of reversal is simple. In this present life, if we reject the lure of ease and power and wholeheartedly pursue the greater goal of love, we will have blessing in the life to come. Jesus came to make this reversal possible.

**The principle of separation (Luke 16:26).** After having sought only to grab comfort at any cost in his earthly life, the rich man now wished to also acquire it in the afterlife. Yet the principle of separation is that this life is the time to obey God and accept His invitation to rewards in the afterlife.

## A PRINCIPLE OF REVELATION—Luke 16:27-29

**Demanding of God (Luke 16:27-28).** In calling for Lazarus to be raised from the dead, the rich man was insisting that God bless his brothers with a uniquely compelling witness to the truth. He wanted it to be easy for them. He simply wanted his brothers to receive a free pass that would keep them out of hell. Abraham showed the rich man that his brothers already had sufficient evidence; they could receive salvation if they had faith.

**Sufficient revelation (Luke 16:29).** The Pharisees loved money and yet pretended to be devoted keepers of God's commandments. Jesus made their condemnation apparent by identifying them with the rich man and his brothers in the parable; they had not truly followed what Moses commanded.

## HINTS OF THE HIGHEST REVELATION—Luke 16:30-31

**The temptation of easy repentance (Luke 16:30).** The rich man thought a simple offer of eternal happiness by a spirit from the afterlife would make his brothers repent. In this parable, Jesus was about to foreshadow His coming resurrection. He was about to hint that our blindness to God is so deep that even one returning from death would not cause us to seek healing.

**The raising of Jesus foreshadowed (Luke 16:31).** Most of the Pharisees continued in disbelief after Jesus was raised from the dead. The rich man's idea that people would believe if someone rose from the grave bearing good news was exposed as false.

—*Derek Leman.*

# QUESTIONS

1. Why do some doubt that this is a parable and instead contend that it describes real events?
2. What did tellers of parables usually use them for?
3. How did the Pharisees compare to the rich man?
4. What commandments were the Pharisees ignoring?
5. How does the phrase "Abraham's bosom" relate Jewish custom?
6. Why is Abraham's table important in a description of the afterlife?
7. What is the effect of Jesus' reference to crumbs of food and drops of water?
8. What is essential for evaluating differing views about hell?
9. What is the principle of separation?
10. How did Jesus hint about His resurrection?

—*Derek Leman.*

## PRACTICAL POINTS

1. Regardless of whether they are rich or poor, people have a tendency to rely on their own resources (Luke 16:19; cf. 18:24-25).
2. Only those who humble themselves will receive the Lord's mercy that brings eternal life (16:20-22).
3. Heaven is a real place where God's comfort and peace are always present.
4. Hell is a literal place where there is continuous torment for the unbeliever (vss. 23-26).
5. Those who deliberately reject the Word of God set themselves on a course that is very difficult to leave (vss. 27-31).

—Paul R. Bawden.

## RESEARCH AND DISCUSSION

1. Outward appearances do not fool God; why do they confuse us so easily?
2. Why is it so easy for a person of wealth to bypass the true eternal riches in Jesus Christ (Luke 16:24-25; cf. I Tim. 6:10)?
3. There are two ways in life (Matt. 7:13-14); what clues show the ways the rich man and Lazarus chose?
4. Do you think Abraham's bosom is the same as heaven? Was the place the rich man suffered the same as hell?
5. How can a believer be a better witness for Christ both to the wealthy and the poor?
6. Why did the resurrection of Christ not convince unbelievers of the truth?

—Paul R. Bawden.

## Golden Text Illuminated

**"If they hear not Moses and the prophets, neither will they be persuaded, though one rose from the dead" (Luke 16:31).**

Is it not tempting to seek and trust in riches in this life? It is easy to be deceived into thinking that the point of life is to gain material prosperity. This sort of message is all around us. People who live this way are plentiful, but the message is wrong. Under God's reign and dominion, earthly riches will not count toward eternal reward. True riches is eternal life through Jesus Christ.

The golden text points to the blindness that can overtake the human heart on this point. Abraham remarked to the rich man that the witness of Moses and the prophets in the Word of God is sufficient to realize the realities of heaven and hell and what true riches are. Sending the dead back to warn them would do no good if they were unwilling to listen to God's Word. Earthly wealth is dangerous because it can lead us to ignore our need for repentance and faith in Jesus Christ.

Jesus gave a powerful warning in describing the fate of the rich man and Lazarus. Earthly wealth can blind us to our need for true riches, which is God's gift of eternal life through faith in Jesus Christ. The rich man ended up with eternal regret. The poor man, Lazarus, ended up with eternal comfort. Decisions and priorities in this life have a bearing on the next. Let us understand what true riches are.

—Jeff VanGoethem.

LESSON 10 — FEBRUARY 2, 2014

## Scripture Lesson Text

**JAS. 1:19** Wherefore, my beloved brethren, let every man be swift to hear, slow to speak, slow to wrath:

**20 For the wrath of man worketh not the righteousness of God.**

21 Wherefore lay apart all filthiness and superfluity of naughtiness, and receive with meekness the engrafted word, which is able to save your souls.

**22 But be ye doers of the word, and not hearers only, deceiving your own selves.**

23 For if any be a hearer of the word, and not a doer, he is like unto a man beholding his natural face in a glass:

**24 For he beholdeth himself, and goeth his way, and straightway forgetteth what manner of man he was.**

25 But whoso looketh into the perfect law of liberty, and continueth *therein,* he being not a forgetful hearer, but a doer of the work, this man shall be blessed in his deed.

**26 If any man among you seem to be religious, and bridleth not his tongue, but deceiveth his own heart, this man's religion *is* vain.**

27 Pure religion and undefiled before God and the Father is this, To visit the fatherless and widows in their affliction, *and* to keep himself unspotted from the world.

Adult Bible Class

# Hear and Do the Word

## Lesson: James 1:19-27

Read: James 1:19-27

TIME: about A.D. 44

PLACE: from Jerusalem

**GOLDEN TEXT**—"Be ye doers of the word, and not hearers only, deceiving your own selves" (James 1:22).

## Lesson Exposition

The letter of James shows a few marks of being addressed to specific groups of believing Jews outside the land of Israel. James applied the wisdom of Jesus, Proverbs, and the Law of Moses to their problems.

### THE SPEECH OF THE SAVED—Jas. 1:19-21

**Redemptive conversation (Jas. 1:19).** The word "wherefore" directs us to what James had just stated in verse 18—that the Father appointed us to be saved. The Father sends His good things down for the sake of His children (vs. 17), including Jesus, whom He sent to rescue us from sin and death.

That train of thought led James to declare that we therefore must live as people appointed for the life to come. He recognized that we humans perpetuate sin and death largely by our words and our anger.

James's original readers were believing Jews outside the land of Israel (Jas. 1:1) who faced serious trials (vs. 2), probably because they were in areas with many nonbelieving Jews (cf. 2:6-7). Many readers also were poor (1:9).

Being "swift to hear" (Jas. 1:19) is one of the greatest pieces of wisdom we can apply to our conversation. The desire of the human heart is to be heard. Selfish conversation looks to be heard, not to listen. Being "slow to speak" is wisdom applicable in many situations. Quick, shallow answers to people's problems come from those who are overly eager to speak. Love-destroying self-centeredness comes from those who are keen to force others to listen.

**Destructive anger (Jas. 1:20).** The one who is angry assumes the right to judge others, to pronounce sentence, and to cause hurt. Anger often divides people, making love difficult or impossible.

In contrast, the righteousness of God is welcoming and heals people.

**Engrafted commandments (Jas. 1:21).** We should have a gentleness that comes from our security in being saved. We should conduct our conversation to help others. Many readers may interpret James 1:21 as introducing a new topic. Yet it may be that James simply regarded angry and selfish conversation as filthy, superfluous, vain, and naughty.

## THE LAW KEEPING OF THE BLESSED—Jas. 1:22-25

**Purposeful application (Jas. 1:22).** Many of the teachings in the letter of James can also be found in the words of Jesus, and 1:22 is a clear example. Jesus knew well the tendencies people have to take the easy part of faith and ignore the task of reforming their lives.

**Hypocritical affirmation (Jas. 1:23-24).** This parable illustrates a person looking into the words of God, comparing them to his own actions and attitudes, seeing the inconsistency there, and yet walking away unchanged.

The words of God in Scripture are like a mirror, showing us what we are supposed to be. We should not forget the discrepancies we see between our own actions and attitudes and those of Jesus.

**Blessed law keeping (Jas. 1:25).** Two new things are introduced in this verse. First, James taught that there is a "law of liberty." Second, he indicated that those who did as he had been teaching—keeping the teachings of the word with action—would be blessed.

According to Jesus, the two greatest commandments are from Deuteronomy 6:4-5 and Leviticus 19:18. In whatever manner the Old Testament laws could be interpreted, they must always reflect these as the highest priority. James referred specifically to the concept of Jesus' teaching on love and called this way of interpreting the Law the "law of liberty" (Jas. 1:25).

What did James mean that the one who lives according to a proper interpretation of the law will be "blessed in his deed" (Jas. 1:25)? In 5:16 James taught that the prayers of those who live by righteousness are more powerful than the prayers of the less righteous. In 3:18 he explained that those who live by the law interpreted through love have peace in their hearts.

## THE RELIGION OF THE UNDEFILED—Jas. 1:26-27

**Vain religion (Jas. 1:26).** Many aspects of a person can be controlled rather easily. The tongue, however, is difficult, for our words often reveal our emotions and attitudes.

**Pure religion (Jas. 1:27).** From the actions of Jesus, James taught the ultimate example of godliness. Jesus said the highest form of service is to those who cannot repay (Luke 14:14).

James, through this letter, was teaching his disciples outside the land of Israel a way of life. His teachings are just as valid and needed today.

—Derek Leman.

# QUESTIONS

1. How does James 1:19 look back to what had just been said in verses 17-18?
2. Who was James writing to?
3. Why is being "swift to hear" (vs. 19) rarely practiced?
4. When a person becomes angry, what particular right does he erroneously feel belongs to him?
5. What good does listening do?
6. What are some different ways of interpreting "filthiness" (vs. 21)?
7. How does the illustration of a person needing to look in a mirror relate to looking into the commandments of God?
8. What other important teaching sheds light on the exact meaning of "law of liberty" (vs. 25)?
9. What sorts of blessings might verse 25 refer to?
10. How can a person's speech unmask his hypocrisy?

—Derek Leman.

Adult Bible Class

## PRACTICAL POINTS

1. Being a good listener is the work of a wise person (Jas. 1:19).
2. Only God is capable of truly fair judgments (vs. 20).
3. Let the Word of God reform your attitude and demeanor (vs. 21).
4. Hearing God's Word but not acting on it is harmful to our spiritual well-being (vs. 22).
5. Blemishes on our spiritual lives often stand out to those around us like an unkempt physical appearance (vss. 23-24).
6. A hearer and doer of God's Word finds fulfillment in ministering to those in need while keeping his life pure before God (vss. 25-27).

—Paul R. Bawden.

## RESEARCH AND DISCUSSION

1. Why might a person's words display who he really is in his character (Jas. 1:19)?
2. Why is it so important to avoid becoming angry (vs. 20)?
3. How should we respond when we have been wronged by another person (Jas. 1:21; cf. Rom. 12:19-21)?
4. Why would a casual reading of Scripture not bring change into a believer's life (Jas. 1:22)?
5. What are some ways through which we can allow God's Word to more effectively impact us?
6. When we recognize a need in someone's life, is it necessary that we go beyond prayer and comforting words to help him (vs. 27)?

—Paul R. Bawden.

## Golden Text Illuminated

**"Be ye doers of the word, and not hearers only, deceiving your own selves" (James 1:22).**

Our golden text is part of a series of very strong and practical injunctions about living rightly and justly under God.

Being a doer of the word begins with taking in God's Word. We have to look "into the perfect law of liberty" (Jas. 1:25). To walk properly under God, we must hear the Word, and truly know it.

We must act on the Word. Being a doer involves taking in the Word of God and habitually putting it into practice.

Now let us consider this from the other side—failing to be a doer. That makes us hearers only. It is like a man who peers into a mirror, takes a good look at his face, and then later forgets what he looks like. It is a senseless activity. Hearing the Word but not doing it is empty and senseless. It has not accomplished anything in our lives.

This is not true Christian faith. The true Christian faith is living faith. It means restraining anger (Jas. 1:19-20), laying aside filthiness (vs. 21), controlling the tongue (vs. 26), and caring for orphans and widows (vs. 27).

So merely hearing the Word is not enough. It must go further, showing itself in authentic deeds that give evidence we are living justly and righteously under God.

We must not brush off what we hear and learn. This will destroy the practical outworking of the Christian faith in our lives. The book of James challenges us to engage in active obedience.

—Jeff VanGoethem.

LESSON 11  FEBRUARY 9, 2014

## Scripture Lesson Text

**JAS. 2:1** My brethren, have not the faith of our Lord Je′sus Christ, *the Lord* of glory, with respect of persons.

**2 For if there come unto your assembly a man with a gold ring, in goodly apparel, and there come in also a poor man in vile raiment;**

3 And ye have respect to him that weareth the gay clothing, and say unto him, Sit thou here in a good place; and say to the poor, Stand thou there, or sit here under my footstool:

**4 Are ye not then partial in yourselves, and are become judges of evil thoughts?**

5 Hearken, my beloved brethren, Hath not God chosen the poor of this world rich in faith, and heirs of the kingdom which he hath promised to them that love him?

**6 But ye have despised the poor. Do not rich men oppress you, and draw you before the judgment seats?**

7 Do not they blaspheme that worthy name by the which ye are called?

**8 If ye fulfil the royal law according to the scripture, Thou shalt love thy neighbour as thyself, ye do well:**

9 But if ye have respect to persons, ye commit sin, and are convinced of the law as transgressors.

**10 For whosoever shall keep the whole law, and yet offend in one *point*, he is guilty of all.**

11 For he that said, Do not commit adultery, said also, Do not kill. Now if thou commit no adultery, yet if thou kill, thou art become a transgressor of the law.

**12 So speak ye, and so do, as they that shall be judged by the law of liberty.**

13 For he shall have judgment without mercy, that hath shewed no mercy; and mercy rejoiceth against judgment.

Adult Bible Class 51

# Avoid Showing Favoritism

Lesson: James 2:1-13

Read: James 2:1-13

TIME: about A.D. 44      PLACE: from Jerusalem

**GOLDEN TEXT**—"If ye fulfil the royal law according to the scripture, Thou shalt love thy neighbour as thyself, ye do well" (James 2:8).

## Lesson Exposition

**UNLOVING PARTIALITY—Jas. 2:1-4**

**Faith and partiality (Jas. 2:1-3).** The style of James's letter is not to quote verses directly, but astute Bible readers will find many indirect references to the Law, Jesus' teachings, and Proverbs. The term for "assembly" in verse 2 is the Greek *synagōgē,* suggesting that readers were not yet meeting in separate churches.

The problem that James was addressing in these assemblies was a severe one: the showing of partiality. His words here seem clearly rooted in the laws of Exodus. The illustration depicts a well-dressed, wealthy person being shown honor and a shabby, poor person being dishonored in the seating arrangements of the assembly. The larger issue involves friendship, honor, and respect for all people, regardless of their situation or appearance.

**False judging (Jas. 2:4).** James twice went on to mention the "law of liberty" (1:25; 2:12) and once the "royal law" (2:8). In each case it seems he meant the Law of Moses as rightly interpreted by Jesus. The guiding principles in interpreting the Law are Deuteronomy 6:4-5 and Leviticus 19:18. Thus, it seems that the larger context of Leviticus 19 can be understood as a primer in rightly keeping the Law. Leviticus 19:15, then, settles the matter of personal relations with people of all social statuses. This letter of James is rich with instruction on how to properly apply the Law in our lives.

**RICH POVERTY—Jas. 2:5-7**

**Riches above (Jas. 2:5).** This verse is not a denial that God chooses rich people. This is clear from other verses like 1:10, where the rich are instructed to rejoice in being humbled by God.

The poor were on his mind. The Gospels were probably not yet written when James wrote this letter, but the followers of Jesus memorized and rehearsed His sayings in their gatherings. The sayings we now have in Luke 6:20-26 were likely on James's mind in 2:5. The poor are blessed because there is a life to come in which there will be no poverty. The rich, by contrast, are too easily satisfied with this world's goods.

**Blasphemy in favoritism (Jas. 2:6-7).** Jerusalem leaders were bringing the believers before the elders of the synagogue. Apparently they had not been put out of the synagogue yet, though that time would soon come.

Yet the rebuke of James is directed at the believers. They were being oppressed by rich leaders. How much more evil, then, was it that they neglected their own poor and sought the favor of the rich? Their actions were not in keeping with the glory of the name by which they were called.

### LAW-KEEPING LOVE—Jas. 2:8-13

**Proper interpretation of law (Jas. 2:8).** Why did James cite Leviticus 19:18? It is because the sin he was addressing lay in the realm of social relationships. All of the commandments in the law that deal with relationships between people are summed up in Leviticus 19:18. Anyone who studies the law with this insight will find that it clarifies the meaning of everything in the law.

Why does James 2:8 refer to this as the "royal law"? We do not read this expression anywhere else in the Bible. It could be "royal" because, in a sense, it is a king among the commandments. This could be compared to the way we use the word "chief." We might say, "To love one's neighbor as oneself is the chief commandment."

**Transgressors (Jas. 2:9-10).** Jesus said that some of His opponents were guilty of a sinful way of law keeping. They emphasized lesser matters of the law and neglected justice, mercy, and faith (Matt. 23:23). Paul said that no matter what great things a person accomplishes by and for the faith, without love they are worthless (I Cor. 13:1-3). It could be that the very sin James was rebuking the Jewish believers for (being unloving toward their fellow poor) was the one point of the law that makes one guilty even if all the rest are kept.

**Priorities (Jas. 2:11).** James's point in this verse is a sharp one. It was meant to be read as a strong chastisement for foolishness in thinking about the law. Can a murderer claim righteousness because he at least did not commit adultery? We would laugh at the idea. Yet the Jewish believing community outside Israel did not see its own blindness.

**The law of liberty (Jas. 2:12-13).** We must all appear before the Judge (I Cor. 3:13-15; II Cor. 5:10). By faith in the gospel a person is justified now; that is, he is righteous in Christ. Nevertheless, in the future each person must make an appearance before the Judge. The basis of that judgment will be deeds—whether or not we were doers of the law of liberty (cf. Jas. 1:25), thus showing whether our faith was genuine or not.

—*Derek Leman.*

# QUESTIONS

1. What kind of references to other Scriptures does one usually find in James?
2. What is the possible reason James 2:2 uses the word "assembly" rather than "church"?
3. What larger issue lies behind the illustration on seating arrangements in verses 2-3?
4. How is Leviticus 19 significant in understanding James's view of the law?
5. How do we know that James did not intend to deny hope for the rich?
6. How could James say God selected the poor to be rich in faith?
7. What might have been happening that led James to speak of the rich oppressing his readers?
8. Why was James's rebuke directed at believers?
9. To what does the "royal law" (vs. 8) likely refer? Why?
10. Why do believers need to be mindful of the final judgment?

—*Derek Leman.*

Adult Bible Class

## PRACTICAL POINTS

1. Preferring the rich over the poor is a worldly and sinful attitude (Jas. 2:1-4).
2. A man's true wealth lies in the amount of faith he has (vs. 5).
3. The rich have a tendency to rely on themselves, making it much more difficult to honor God (vss. 6-7).
4. We are not to show love based on a person's merit but only because God first loved us (vss. 8-9).
5. If we are guilty of any sin, we are guilty of breaking the whole law (vss. 10-11).
6. The Lord repays our mercy with His mercy, but our judgment earns His judgment (vss. 12-13).

—Paul R. Bawden.

## RESEARCH AND DISCUSSION

1. Why is God so against showing partiality? What does this tell us about God's unconditional love (Jas. 2:1-3; cf. I John 4:9-11)?
2. Why is it so easy to honor someone who is wealthy and look down on someone who does not have many possessions in this world (Jas. 2:4-6)?
3. How does showing partiality break God's law just as adultery and murder break God's law (vss. 7-11)?
4. How can a follower of Christ have the same honoring attitude toward people that Christ had (cf. Matt. 9:35-36)?
5. As Christians, should we fear passing judgment on others (Jas. 2:12-13)?

—Paul R. Bawden.

## Golden Text Illuminated

**"If ye fulfil the royal law according to the scripture, Thou shalt love thy neighbour as thyself, ye do well" (James 2:8).**

In this unit we are concerned with living justly under the reign of God.

In no greater way will this be manifested than in how we treat other people. We cannot fulfill the Word of God in our lives by going into the world looking out for number one or by living to seek the approval of others. We have a God-given duty to treat people as God commands us.

People who come to faith in Jesus Christ and enter the church come from all walks of life and from all backgrounds. There is to be no favoritism in the preaching of the gospel and within the body of Christ. We minister to anyone and everyone; all are to be welcomed. There is no question that there are occasions when the church has failed on this point.

James refers to the "royal law," a probable reference to the highest rule of God's Word, which, after the command to love God, is to "love thy neighbour as thyself." This is the essential standard of the social dimension of our lives under God. And of course this is utterly incompatible with showing favoritism, particularly within the body of Christ. How can we diminish someone whom Christ has received? How can we exalt anyone other than the Lord Jesus, who is the precious Saviour? We are to extend to all, in and out of the body of Christ, acceptance, consideration, love, justice, kindness, and friendship. This is what fulfills the Word of God.

—Jeff VanGoethem.

LESSON 12　　　　　　　　　　　　　　　　　　FEBRUARY 16, 2014

# Scripture Lesson Text

**JAS. 2:14** What *doth it* profit, my brethren, though a man say he hath faith, and have not works? can faith save him?

**15 If a brother or sister be naked, and destitute of daily food,**

16 And one of you say unto them, Depart in peace, be *ye* warmed and filled; notwithstanding ye give them not those things which are needful to the body; what *doth it* profit?

**17 Even so faith, if it hath not works, is dead, being alone.**

18 Yea, a man may say, Thou hast faith, and I have works: shew me thy faith without thy works, and I will shew thee my faith by my works.

**19 Thou believest that there is one God; thou doest well: the devils also believe, and tremble.**

20 But wilt thou know, O vain man, that faith without works is dead?

**21 Was not A'bra-ham our father justified by works, when he had offered I'saac his son upon the altar?**

22 Seest thou how faith wrought with his works, and by works was faith made perfect?

**23 And the scripture was fulfilled which saith, A'bra-ham believed God, and it was imputed unto him for righteousness: and he was called the Friend of God.**

24 Ye see then how that by works a man is justified, and not by faith only.

**25 Likewise also was not Ra'hab the harlot justified by works, when she had received the messengers, and had sent *them* out another way?**

26 For as the body without the spirit is dead, so faith without works is dead also.

Adult Bible Class

# Show Your Faith by Your Works

## Lesson: James 2:14-26

Read: James 2:14-26

TIME: about A.D. 44      PLACE: from Jerusalem

**GOLDEN TEXT**—"As the body without the spirit is dead, so faith without works is dead also" (James 2:26).

# Lesson Exposition

## THE PROBLEM OF FAITHLESS FAITH—Jas. 2:14-17

**A false claim (Jas. 2:14).** There are two primary interpretations of works in Paul's teaching, and regardless of which is followed, James meant something different.

A traditional understanding of "works of the law" in Paul's teaching was that Jews were trying to earn salvation by merit. James was not talking about works as a sufficient basis to merit salvation. Many commentators have come to think "works of the law" means the idea that Jews are saved by being Jewish. Paul was proving that Gentiles did not have to become Jewish through circumcision to be saved. James was not talking about works in that way, either.

The works James was talking about are expressions of love for God and neighbor that spring from true faith. They are works of mercy, not works of merit. The gospel of Jesus may have been latched on to by certain individuals as a handy new excuse for their faithless outlook and conduct.

**A false profession (Jas. 2:15-16).** The person who would send away the desperately needy brother with religious sentiments is a miserly fool. Such a person is double minded, since he professes caring.

**A false dichotomy (Jas. 2:17).** It is simple to separate faith and works of loving-kindness, says James 2:17. What makes this kind of faith "dead" is that it is "alone." Just as there is no genuine compassion without action (vs. 16), so there is no real faith that is faithless toward God.

## THE USELESSNESS OF FAITHLESS FAITH—Jas. 2:18-20

**Impossibility (Jas. 2:18).** A person with works of love can demonstrate that he engaged in deeds of love by faith, but a person who simply claims to have faith cannot demonstrate something that is only internal.

**Futility (Jas. 2:19).** Demonic powers have much true knowledge of God. A number of events in the New Testament include glimpses of the right beliefs of demons. If demons have correct belief even about what the message of salvation is and yet remain workers of evil, no one could imagine that they are saved. So James has proved beyond doubt that correct belief separated from correct action is useless.

**Rebuke (Jas. 2:20).** What sort of person attempts to separate faith and works? The answer is a "vain man."

This man is vain in the sense of Ecclesiastes 1:2: "all is vanity." In this usage, "vanity" means something that appears to be real but is not.

## THE REFUTATION OF FAITHLESS FAITH—Jas. 2:21-26

**The faithful faith of Abraham (Jas. 2:21-22).** James knew the Abraham stories perfectly well, and yet his inspired conclusion was that Abraham was justified by works. It is important to remember that works here means works of love.

In the famous story of Genesis 22, a cornerstone of belief in Judaism, there is a turning point in God's relationship with Abraham. After seeing Abraham's willingness to sacrifice Isaac, the Lord told him, "Now I know that thou fearest God" (vs. 12).

**The fulfillment of faith (Jas. 2:23).** The Bible often works on the pattern of promise and fulfillment. According to James, Genesis 15:6 and 22:12-17 follow that pattern. In Genesis 15:6 Abraham was already declared right with God, or justified. The fulfillment came in Abraham's action of love for God.

**Justification by complete faith (Jas. 2:24).** James had already brought up the final judgment in verses 12-13. Belief in Jesus does not cause anyone to escape finally appearing before the Judge. In that court, works of love will be at the heart of a verdict of righteousness.

Faith and works are inseparable. He who believes, works; and he who truly works, believes.

**An example of complete faith (Jas. 2:25).** Rahab was a Canaanite, not an Israelite. She is an unlikely example of righteous faith. Her story is also perfect for illustration because, as a Canaanite, she was doomed by God's decree to death.

What clinched her salvation was an action. She demonstrated her faith with the right action.

**A final illustration (Jas. 2:26).** The final illustration James used for faithless faith is of a body after the spirit has departed. A believer without works of love is like a dead body. He has not truly been begotten by the word of truth.

—*Derek Leman.*

## QUESTIONS

1. What are two interpretations of the "works of the law" in Paul's writings?
2. How are "works" in James 2 different from Paul's use of the term?
3. How do we know that the idea of faith without works was not new in James's time?
4. Why is faith that does not result in good works described as being dead?
5. What evidence is there that demons possess much true knowledge about God?
6. What does "vain" mean in verse 20?
7. How does the pattern of promise and fulfillment relate to Abraham's justification in Genesis 15 and 22?
8. How do works bear on final judgment?
9. What in Rahab's background makes her such a pertinent example?
10. How does a corpse provide an analogy for faith without works?

—*Derek Leman.*

# PRACTICAL POINTS

1. True faith in the Lord will have evidence that it is genuine faith (Jas. 2:14-17).
2. Faith without works is just knowledge; we are to believe, or trust, in a way that works (vss. 18-20).
3. Abraham demonstrated that he had faith when he offered his son Isaac on the altar (vss. 21-22).
4. God called faithful Abraham His friend (vss. 23-24).
5. Rahab had such faith in the Lord that she risked her life (vs. 25).
6. As a person's spirit gives life to his body, his works show his living faith (vs. 26).

—Paul R. Bawden.

# RESEARCH AND DISCUSSION

1. What is faith (Heb. 11:1), and why is it necessary to have faith in the Lord for salvation apart from any works one can do (Jas. 2:14; cf. Rom. 4:1-5; Eph. 2:8-9)?
2. Why is it also necessary for believers in Christ to live by faith (Heb. 11:6; cf. II Cor. 4:15-18; 5:7)?
3. What is the basis for faith in the Lord for salvation and for daily living (Heb. 6:13-20)?
4. Why do so many unsaved people think that works are necessary to receive eternal life, and why is it so hard for them to understand that their good deeds do not impress God (cf. II Cor. 4:3-4)?
5. How can believers in the power of the Holy Spirit demonstrate by their works that they are true followers of Jesus Christ?

—Paul R. Bawden.

# Golden Text Illuminated

**"As the body without the spirit is dead, so faith without works is dead also" (James 2:26).**

We are to show our faith by our works (Jas. 2:18). How faith and works work together is at the essence of New Testament Christianity. We must have a genuine faith, which will show itself in works. What does this mean?

First of all, if we claim to have faith in Christ but there are no good and godly works manifesting obedience to God, then our faith is dead.

The implication is that true faith will manifest itself in works and deeds of obedience to God.

A second point to be made is that James does not give us a formula of exactly which works must be present, how long they must be present, and in what order they must come! James simply gives us a sound and true principle so that we may judge ourselves (I Pet. 4:17) and so that we may understand that a mere profession of Christianity, if it produces no change, is not the real thing.

Another point to be made is that the Christian faith is first of all a religion of the heart. We believe in the Lord Jesus in our hearts. From this it becomes a religion of life and living.

Finally, James is not teaching that we depend on our works for salvation. Salvation is by grace alone, through faith alone, in Christ alone. No works or deeds of our own can add to what He did for us on the cross. Although they go along with salvation, good works do not cause it.

—Jeff VanGoethem.

LESSON 13 — FEBRUARY 23, 2014

## Scripture Lesson Text

**JAS. 3:1** My brethren, be not many masters, knowing that we shall receive the greater condemnation.

**2 For in many things we offend all. If any man offend not in word, the same *is* a perfect man, *and* able also to bridle the whole body.**

3 Behold, we put bits in the horses' mouths, that they may obey us; and we turn about their whole body.

**4 Behold also the ships, which though *they be* so great, and *are* driven of fierce winds, yet are they turned about with a very small helm, whithersoever the governor listeth.**

5 Even so the tongue is a little member, and boasteth great things. Behold, how great a matter a little fire kindleth!

**6 And the tongue *is* a fire, a world of iniquity: so is the tongue among our members, that it defileth the whole body, and setteth on fire the course of nature; and it is set on fire of hell.**

7 For every kind of beasts, and of birds, and of serpents, and of things in the sea, is tamed, and hath been tamed of mankind:

**8 But the tongue can no man tame; *it is* an unruly evil, full of deadly poison.**

9 Therewith bless we God, even the Father; and therewith curse we men, which are made after the similitude of God.

**10 Out of the same mouth proceedeth blessing and cursing. My brethren, these things ought not so to be.**

11 Doth a fountain send forth at the same place sweet *water* and bitter?

**12 Can the fig tree, my brethren, bear olive berries? either a vine, figs? so *can* no fountain both yield salt water and fresh.**

# Control Your Speech

Lesson: James 3:1-12

Read: James 3:1-12

TIME: about A.D. 44      PLACE: from Jerusalem

---

**GOLDEN TEXT**—"Out of the same mouth proceedeth blessing and cursing. My brethren, these things ought not so to be" (James 3:10).

---

## Lesson Exposition

**SINS OF SPEAKING—Jas. 3:1-2**

**The danger for teachers (Jas. 3:1).** James's injunction that few should be masters relates to the desire in many of us to be teachers or advice-givers to others. In a Jewish setting, disciples would refer to teachers with deference, using titles such as "Master" and "Father." In modern churches there are titles for leaders that also indicate deference. It is not uncommon for us to desire the seemingly easy and self-glorifying aspects of leadership.

Yet we should not assume James's warning applies only to teachers. In everyday situations and conversation, we face the temptation to be a master over others. We are quick to give advice. We judge as if we had authority.

Why will the judgment on a teacher require more? Jesus taught us the principle of the final judgment that "unto whomsoever much is given, of him shall be much required" (Luke 12:48). Further, those who teach end up using many words to do their task.

**The struggle for all of us (Jas. 3:2).** Godliness means a path of struggle to increasingly master our bodies. James had already reminded his readers of the coming judgment. Being mindful of this, we see how our lower urges continually drive us to do wrong. Godliness is by faith and is impossible without grace, but it is also work.

**ILLUSTRATIONS OF THE TONGUE'S POWER—Jas. 3:3-8**

**Bridling speech (Jas. 3:3).** The tongue is a little thing, and words are small; but they are powerful.

The capacity of our actions to affect others and the world around us should not be measured in ounces, but in terms of horsepower. The strength of horses is legendary. Yet all this power can be controlled with a small rod in the mouth of the animal.

Even so, if we could control our tongues, we could master our entire body. The power of our true nature is expressed in words, too often spoken hastily. Hidden inner selfishness comes out in words. Though they are small, we wreak havoc with them.

**Overcoming momentum (Jas. 3:4).** The "governor," or pilot, is the person steering a ship by using a helm to turn the rudder. The direction is controlled by the small movements he makes. The governor of speech, which is each one of us, holds the helm and has the power to steer relationships either for good or for evil.

**Careless speech (Jas. 3:5-6).** The tongue boasts. The excitability of a speaker is like the ease with which a flame catches and spreads. What starts small turns large quickly. Words are volatile, like fire. They also damage like fire.

The likening of the tongue to a small flame brings to mind the innumerable sins of the tongue that make life in society like hell. The tongue is the motor driving the sins that lead to hell.

**The untamable tongue (Jas. 3:7-8).** Humanity can boast of many accomplishments. Yet the taming of the tongue is beyond us.

Did James literally mean that no human being can be completely righteous with his words? Some theologies believe we are able not to sin, while others hold to the impossibility of complete holiness. Regardless of which theology is correct, we cannot lower our goal based on impossibility. James's intent in saying the tongue cannot be tamed was to awaken in us a desire to be complete. If we can tame our tongue, we will know that our inner person is truly renewed.

## PURITY OF SPEECH—Jas. 3:9-12

**Positive power (Jas. 3:9-10).** Up till now, James's instructions about speech have been entirely negative. Yet now he referred to the positive power of speech.

One of the purest forms of love is appreciation. Another is willing good for someone. The word "blessing" can include both. Blessing is the way of promoting with speech everything that is good and pure.

By contrast, cursing God is unthinkable—though there are those who do so. With people, both scorn and harmful intent come readily to our speech. We suppose our words can be secret, but the Judge always hears them.

**Blessing and cursing (Jas. 3:11-12).** James described the hypocrisy of evil speech. Most people praise God or some higher power. Yet, as everyone knows, humanity is full of evil speech. Shouting, cursing, belittling, complaining, criticizing, and rejecting words are all around us.

We observe that a spring sends either brackish water, or pure water. No spring alternates. Likewise, we observe that a tree is predictable in its produce. We expect olives or figs, and we get them. Why are people not as reliable as mere trees? Yet God and people are continually disappointed by the fruit of our lips—our tree, as it were. Let us use our mouths to give life and the love that is needed.

—*Derek Leman.*

# QUESTIONS

1. What titles were given to teachers in James's time? What did this show?
2. Why should the warning about few being masters not be limited to the position of teacher?
3. Why will teachers be judged more strictly?
4. How does the picture of a horse and bit illustrate the power of speech?
5. What do hasty and careless words reveal about us?
6. In what way is the tongue given to boasting?
7. Why is the tongue likened to the fire of hell?
8. If no one can gain complete control over the tongue, why try?
9. What are the types of blessing, and why is blessing a force for good in the world?
10. What lesson about speech can we glean from trees?

—*Derek Leman.*

## PRACTICAL POINTS

1. Our words show our true character (Jas. 3:1-2).
2. Small things can often be used to exert control over people in unimaginable ways (vss. 3-4).
3. The tongue, although small, has incredible power to defile a person's body, his reputation, and his future (vss. 5-6).
4. The damage done by idle words can be long-lasting and far-reaching (vss. 7-8).
5. A person's tongue can do either good or evil; put yours to work for God (vss. 9-10).
6. Resolve that in the Holy Spirit's power, you will speak words that build people up, not tear them down (vss. 11-12).

—Paul R. Bawden.

## RESEARCH AND DISCUSSION

1. Why did James warn people to be cautious about seeking positions of authority in the church (Jas. 3:1; cf. Luke 12:48)?
2. How might a person's speech reveal whether he is maturing in Christ?
3. What seemingly small attitudes and actions can elevate people to positions over others?
4. How can the tongue have such a controlling influence on a person's own life or the lives of others?
5. What is wrong with the heart of mankind (cf. Mark 7:21-23)?
6. How does accepting Christ as Saviour bring a change to one's vocabulary (Eph. 5:18-21)?

—Paul R. Bawden.

## Golden Text Illuminated

"Out of the same mouth proceedeth blessing and cursing. My brethren, these things ought not so to be" (James 3:10).

Our golden text teaches us important truths. Let us first consider how our capacity for speech can be used for evil. James says it can be used for "cursing." He points out the hypocrisy of this behavior. One day we praise God, and the next day we curse man. This does not add up. Man is made in God's image, so to attack others is to attack God's creation and rule.

We should also see that much good can be done with our ability to speak. The capacity for speech has been given by God, after all! It has the power to bless others and bless God. The tongue can be used for such things as praise, worship, and prayer. So this text is not calling on us to be silent; it is asking us to recognize the need for care, because we can do both good and evil with our mouths.

It is interesting that throughout the third chapter James spends no time giving some kind of process or formula for subduing the tongue. The epistle does not tell us exactly how to do it. Rather, it seems to imply that our speech will tend to reflect what we are—that is, the true nature of our spiritual condition. The key to controlling our speech, then, is putting our whole lives under God's control. This will lead us to use our speech for good and not for evil, to bless and not to curse. May the Lord help us use this powerful gift for His glory!

—Jeff VanGoethem.

# PARAGRAPHS ON PLACES AND PEOPLE

## BETHLEHEM

This city, located about five miles south of Jerusalem, is known as the birthplace of Jesus. We learn in Luke 2 that Joseph and his expectant wife, Mary, traveled to Bethlehem, "the city of David," to participate in a census decreed by Caesar Augustus, as Joseph "was of the house and lineage of David" (vs. 4). It was there that Mary "brought forth her firstborn son" (vs. 7).

Bethlehem is identified in the Old Testament as the place where Jacob buried his wife Rachel (Gen. 35:19). The area later became a center for the tribe of Judah, which included Jesse, the father of David. A young David was anointed by the Prophet Samuel at that locale (I Sam. 16:1-13). David later became king over a united Israel.

## NAZARETH

The city of Nazareth is located in northern Israel in the region of Galilee. It was the site of the annunciation, in which the Angel Gabriel appeared to Mary and revealed to her that she would give birth to Jesus, the "Son of the Highest" (Luke 1:32). Jesus was often referred to as Jesus of Nazareth because He lived in the city during His youth.

Some negative depictions of the inhabitants of Nazareth can be found in the New Testament. When Philip told Nathanael that he had found the Messiah, Nathanael replied, "Can there any good thing come out of Nazareth?" (John 1:46). Even Jesus' own siblings did not believe in Him during His ministry (7:5). On another occasion, Jesus said, "A prophet is not without honour, but in his own country, and among his own kin, and in his own house" (Mark 6:4).

## CAESAR AUGUSTUS

Gaius Julius Caesar Octavius was the first emperor of the Roman Empire, ruling from 27 B.C. until his death in A.D. 14. Born Gaius Octavius in 63 B.C., he was adopted posthumously by his great-uncle, Gaius Julius Caesar, through a last will and testament in 44 B.C.

The title Augustus, meaning "venerable" or "revered," was bestowed on him by the Roman senate upon his rise to power.

We read in the Gospel of Luke, "There went out a decree from Caesar Augustus, that all the world should be taxed" (2:1). A census was to be conducted throughout the land of Palestine, which was under Roman rule. Joseph traveled to his hometown of Bethlehem, along with Mary, to comply with this mandate. It was during this time that Mary gave birth to Jesus, fulfilling the prophecy that the Messiah would be born in Bethlehem (Mic. 5:2).

## ZACHARIAS

Zacharias (or Zechariah) is identified in the Gospel of Luke as "a certain priest . . . of the course of Abia" (1:5). He and his wife, Elisabeth, became the parents of John the Baptist. The account tells us, "They were both righteous before God" (vs. 6).

Zacharias was performing his priestly duties in the temple at Jerusalem when the Angel Gabriel appeared and told him that his wife, Elisabeth, who was barren, would conceive in her old age. He was instructed to name the child John. Because of his disbelief, Zacharias was made dumb (mute). On the day the child was born, he wrote, "His name is John" (Luke 1:63), at which point he regained the ability to speak.

—Dan Holland.

# Daily Bible Readings for Home Study and Worship

(Readings are for the week previous to the lesson topics.)

1. **December 1.   Jesus' Birth Foretold**
M.—A Covenant with David. Ps. 89:1-7.
T.—God's Faithfulness and Mercy. Ps. 89:19-25.
W.—Higher than All Other Kings. Ps. 89:26-34.
T.—A Promise for the Future. II Sam. 7:18-29.
F.—A Child Named Immanuel. Isa. 7:10-15.
S.—Elisabeth's Blessing. Luke 1:41-45.
S.—The Announcement to Mary. Luke 1:26-40.

2. **December 8.   Mary's Song of Praise**
M.—My Heart Rejoices in the Lord. I Sam. 2:1-10.
T.—Magnifying the Lord Together. Ps. 34:1-8.
W.—Give Thanks to the Lord. Ps. 100:1-5.
T.—Bless the Compassionate Lord. Ps. 103:13-22.
F.—Praise the Gracious and Merciful Lord. Ps. 111:1-10.
S.—The Lord Reigns for All Generations. Ps. 146:1-10.
S.—God Has Done Great Things. Luke 1:46-56.

3. **December 15.   Zacharias's Prophecy**
M.—What Will This Child Become? Luke 1:59-66.
T.—John's Call to Repentance. Luke 3:1-6.
W.—The Fruits of Repentance. Luke 3:7-14.
T.—The Coming Greater One. Luke 3:15-20.
F.—Jesus' Baptism by John. Matt. 3:13-17.
S.—A Prophet and More. Luke 7:18-27.
S.—A Prophet of the Most High. Luke 1:57, 67-79.

4. **December 22.   Jesus' Birth (Christmas)**
M.—A Son Given to the Lord. I Sam. 1:21-28.
T.—The Lord's Blessing on His People. Num. 6:22-27.
W.—A Great Light. Isa. 9:1-5.
T.—A Ruler from Bethlehem. Mic. 5:1-5.
F.—God's Deliverance and Mercy. Ps. 18:46-50.
S.—The Fullness of Time. Gal. 4:1-7.
S.—The Birth of Jesus in Bethlehem. Luke 2:1-17.

5. **December 29.   Jesus Presented in the Temple**
M.—Abiding by the Law. Luke 2:21-24.
T.—Circumcised on the Eighth Day. Lev. 12:1-5.
W.—An Offering to the Lord. Lev. 12:6-8.
T.—The Consolation of Israel. Isa. 40:1-5.
F.—Comfort and Compassion from the Lord. Isa. 49:8-13.
S.—A Light to the Nations. Isa. 42:1-7.
S.—Presentation in the Temple. Luke 2:25-38.

6. **January 5.   Honoring the Sabbath**
M.—God Is Still Working. John 5:2-17.
T.—A Day of Thanksgiving. Ps. 92:1-8.
W.—A Day of Rest. Exod. 16:22-30.
T.—A Day of Remembrance. Deut. 5:11-15.
F.—A Holy Convocation. Lev. 23:1-8.
S.—A Holy Day. Jer. 17:19-27.
S.—Lord of the Sabbath. Luke 6:1-11.

7. **January 12.   Living as God's People**
M.—God's Righteous Judgment. Ps. 7:7-17.
T.—The Righteous and Upright. Prov. 11:3-11.
W.—Becoming Servants to Righteousness. Rom. 6:16-23.
T.—Living as God's Servants. I Pet. 2:11-17.
F.—Forgiveness and Mercy. Matt. 18:21-35.
S.—Do Not Judge. Luke 6:37-42.
S.—Blessings and Woes. Luke 6:20-31.

8. **January 19.   Showing Humility**
M.—The Fall of the Proud One. Isa. 14:12-20.
T.—Humble Yourself Before the Lord. Jas. 4:7-12.
W.—God Gives Grace to the Humble. I Pet. 5:1-7.
T.—God Gathers the Outcasts. Ps. 147:1-11.
F.—God Lifts the Poor and Needy. Ps. 113:1-9.
S.—God Shows No Partiality. Rom. 2:1-11.
S.—Honor and Disgrace. Luke 14:7-14.

9. **January 26.   Instruction on True Wealth**
M.—Be Generous to the Poor. Deut. 15:7-11.
T.—God Hears the Cry of the Poor. Job 34:17-30.
W.—Feigned Concern for the Poor. John 12:1-8.
T.—Finding True Riches. Luke 19:1-10.
F.—Using Resources Shrewdly. Luke 16:1-9.
S.—Faithful in Small Things. Luke 16:10-18.
S.—From Wealth to Eternal Loss. Luke 16:19-31.

10. **February 2.   Hear and Do the Word**
M.—A People Who Will Not Listen. Jer. 7:21-28.
T.—A Lamp in the Darkness. II Sam. 22:26-31.
W.—The Voice of the Living God. Deut. 5:22-27.
T.—Neither Add nor Take Away. Deut. 4:1-10.
F.—Denying God by Actions. Titus 1:10-16.
S.—Love in Deed and Truth. I John 3:14-20.
S.—Hearers and Doers of the Word. Jas. 1:19-27.

11. **February 9.   Avoid Showing Favoritism**
M.—Judging Rightly and Impartially. Deut. 1:9-18.
T.—Judging on the Lord's Behalf. II Chron. 19:1-7.
W.—Giving Justice to the Weak. Ps. 82:1-8.
T.—Avoid Partiality. Prov. 28:18-22.
F.—God Shows No Partiality. Acts 10:34-43.
S.—Love, Not Partiality. Rom. 13:8-14.
S.—Faith, Not Favoritism. Jas. 2:1-13.

12. **February 16.   Show Your Faith by Your Works**
M.—The Work of Faith. II Thess. 1:3-12.
T.—Faith Derailed by the Love of Money. I Tim. 6:6-12.
W.—Perfecting Incomplete Faith. I Thess. 3:4-13.
T.—An Example of Great Faith. Luke 7:1-10.
F.—A Sinner Saved by Faith. Luke 7:36-50.
S.—Established in the Faith. Col. 2:1-7.
S.—Faith Demonstrated Through Works. Jas. 2:14-26.

13. **February 23.   Control Your Speech**
M.—Lying and Flattering Lips. Ps. 12:1-8.
T.—Words That Intimidate. I Sam. 17:1-11.
W.—Words That Bring Repentance. II Chron. 15:1-12.
T.—Words That Lead to Mourning. Neh. 1:1-11.
F.—Words That Lead to Worship. Gen. 24:42-52.
S.—Wise and Foolish Words. Prov. 18:2-13.
S.—Taming the Tongue. Jas. 3:1-12.